Contents

Preface

Brian Hill's original volume on the European Community, published in 1991, featured the ERM which the UK had just joined, and it also looked forward to the Single Market in 1992.

In this second edition so much has changed apart from the book's title. The United Kingdom quit the ERM; the Single Market is a reality; the wider European Economic Area has been ratified. And yet already four members of it have been accepted as worthy of switching to swell the membership of the EU club.

All these changes are covered in this second edition, as well as the MacSharry Reforms to CAP, the economics of the Social Chapter, and much more ...

Bryan Hurl
Series Editor

The European Union

Second Edition

Previously published as *The European Community*

Brian Hill

Series Editor
Bryan Hurl
Head of Economics, Harrow School

Heinemann

0435330284

Heinemann Educational
a division of Heinemann Publishers (Oxford) Ltd.
Halley Court, Jordan Hill, Oxford OX2 8EJ

OXFORD   LONDON   EDINBURGH
MADRID   ATHENS   BOLOGNA   PARIS
MELBOURNE   SYDNEY   AUCKLAND   SINGAPORE   TOKYO
IBADAN   NAIROBI   HARARE   GABORONE
PORTSMOUTH NH (USA)

First published in 1991 as *The European Community*
Second edition published in 1994 as *The European Union*

98 97 96 95
10 9 8 7 6 5 4 3 2

British Library Cataloguing in Publication Data

A catalogue record for this book is available from the British Library

ISBN 0 435 33028 4

Typeset and illustrated by TechType, Abingdon, Oxon.

Printed and bound in Great Britain by
Athenæum Press Ltd, Gateshead, Tyne & Wear

Acknowledgements

The publishers would like to thank the following for permission to reproduce copyright material:
The Anti-Common Market League for the cartoon on p. 19; H. Armstrong for the table on p. 61; Associated Examining Board for the questions on pp. 22, 38, 70, 82; T. Bailey Forman Ltd. for the article from the *Nottingham Evening Post* on p. 32; Andrew Britton for the article on p. 71; the Central Statistical Office for the data used in the table on p. 80; the Commission of the European Communities for the extract on p. 20; © *Daily Mail*/Solo for the cartoon on p. 5; *The Economist* for the articles on pp. 10, 14–15, 28; Epson Ltd. for the advertisement on pp. 23–5; *The European* for the extract on p. 74; the *Financial Times* for the extract on p. 52; G.A. Geroski for the article on p. 39; Nigel Healey for the table on p. 61; Her Majesty's Stationary Office for the data used in the table on p. 13; Newspaper Publishing plc for the article on p. 67 and the Chris Riddell cartoon on p. 50, both from *The Independent*, and for the extract on p. 83 from the *Independent on Sunday*; Northern Examinations and Assessment Board for the questions on pp. 38, 70; Office for Official Publications of the European Community for the statistics on pp. 3, 11, 31, 35, 46, 57, 65, 66, 75, 85, 86; Oxford and Cambridge Schools Examination Board for questions on pp. 13, 22, 38, 60, 70, 71, 82; © Times Newspapers Ltd. for the articles on pp. 47, 56, 83; University of Cambridge Local Examinations Syndicate for questions on pp. 12, 22, 38, 51, 69; University of London Examinations and Assessment Council for the questions on pp. 12, 38, 51, 60, 70, 83; University of Oxford Delegacy of Local Examinations for the questions on pp. 22, 51, 60, 83; Welsh Joint Education Council for the question on p. 52; the World Bank for data on p. 70.

The publishers have made every effort to contact the correct copyright holders. However, if any material has been incorrectly acknowledged, the publishers would be happy to make the necessary arrangements at the earliest opportunity.

Introduction

Why was the Common Market founded? How does it work? Is it a good thing – especially for the UK? What is likely to happen next?

This book presents the facts in an attempt to help its readers to answer these questions. It begins by tracing the origins of the European Economic Community and examining how it has developed into the European Union.

The economic rationale which underlies this economic integration is the gains to be obtained from the operation of the *law of comparative advantage* in a free market. But this is a 'textbook' theory, so does it really work in the real world? What about imperfections and market failures? In particular, what about the infamous common agricultural policy which makes a mockery of the free market concept? Even if the common market does make everyone better off, as economic theory suggests, are the gains equitably distributed?

The next major policy goal is economic and monetary union – one currency, a European central bank, economic policy determined at the European level. Such a degree of economic integration implies political union, and already the Treaty of Maastricht has made the people of all its member states into Citizens of Europe.

Twice in this century the larger members of the European Union have fought against each other in mutually destructive bloody wars. The human costs are incalculable, the economic costs are small in comparison, yet enormous. The integration of the economies of the twelve member states has welded old enemies into fellow workers and friends; so, by making war amongst its member nations unthinkable, the Union must be a great success. But how does its economic performance in terms of growth compare with that of the USA or Japan?

Is the UK better off as a result of joining the European Union? Is sovereignty given up or shared as integration proceeds? Should the Union be a looser arrangement of sovereign states benefiting from free trade without the shackles of supra-national policies?

Whilst UK politicians argue, European integration progresses inexorably. The end of the process will be a United States of Europe, but *when* remains to be seen. Whether this is a good, bad or sad thing is a matter of opinion. Readers will have to make up their own minds.

Chapter One

Origins of the European Union

'... to establish the foundations of an ever closer union among the European peoples...' Preamble to the Treaty of Rome

What is the European Union, often referred to as 'the Common Market'? It is a combination of twelve West European countries which have decided that their future wellbeing will be enhanced by their union. They are gradually evolving from independent sovereign states to a federation or 'United States of Europe'. This process of integration is both economic and political. *Whilst this book concentrates upon the economic aspects it must not be forgotten that the fundamental forces involved are political, and so, not surprisingly, are controversial.*

In this chapter the forces which have led to the creation of the European Union are outlined briefly and its objectives are analysed against this background. Finally, the EU institutions and the way in which decisions are taken and implemented are examined.

Table 1 opposite gives some basic data on the size and composition of the Community, and comparative data for the United States of America and Japan. As the latter two countries are the Community's major competitors they will be included in several tables throughout the book. Austria, Finland, Norway and Sweden are added because these countries are currently negotiating to join the Community, the expected date of accession being 1 January 1995.

Historical background

At the conclusion of the Second World War, Europe was devastated economically. It was also fundamentally politically divided into a communist East and a capitalist West. The West included Germany and Italy which, with Japan, had fought on one side in the war, whilst the opposing side, the Allies, had included much of the rest of continental Europe in addition to Russia, the USA and the British Empire. Soviet Russia and the USA were much larger and more powerful than any other country. Some West European countries feared that their weakened condition constituted a power vacuum which might be too tempting for their huge eastern neighbour. They came together in defence treaties and to cooperate in economic reconstruction.

In the immediate post-war years many economists and politicians produced plans for a better and more secure future. One of the most influential was the French economist **Jean Monnet**. He envisaged a united Europe in which union would bring peace and prosperity to an area where nationalistic division and rivalry had imposed a tradition of war and misery. He was convinced that a worthwhile future for Europe required economic and political union. The latter had to be a long-term aim since it was unthinkable in the immediate aftermath of bloodshed and bitterness. So he conceived union by degrees, moving gradually from economic cooperation to **economic integration**,

Table 1 The European Community in perspective, 1993

	Area (1000 km²)	Population (millions)	GDP (milliard Ecu)
Belgium	31	10.0	175
Denmark	43	5.2	114
Germany	357	81.6	1610
Greece	132	10.5	63
Spain	505	39.1	407
France	544	58.0	1074
Ireland	70	3.6	39
Italy	301	58.1	850
Luxembourg	3	0.4	9
Netherlands	41	15.4	262
Portugal	92	9.4	65
United Kingdom	244	58.2	798
EUR12	2363	349.7	5466
Austria	84	7.9	125
Finland	337	5.0	91
Norway	324	4.3	104
Sweden	450	8.7	170
Proposed EUR 16	3558	371.2	5956
USA	9373	253.9	5338
Japan	378	123.9	3640

Notes: GDPs at current market prices and exchange rates. Germany is the reunified Germany. The order of countries in this and subsequent tables follows European convention, being alphabetical in the native language of each country; e.g. Germany is Deutschland, Spain is España, etc. Four proposed EC members' data relate to 1992.
Sources: *European Economy, 55*, 1993; *Main Economic Indicators*, OECD, 1993.

ultimately with full **political union** as the desired end.

Monnet's vision was given practical expression through the efforts of skilled politicians such as Conrad Adenauer of Germany, Robert Schuman of France and Paul-Henri Spaak of Belgium. *What role did the UK play?* None! The UK emerged from the war as the only major West European country not to be conquered, greatly weakened but still a world power and still possessing an enormous Empire. The latter absorbed British political attention, particularly as the Empire was being turned into a Commonwealth as its members were given sovereignty over their own-destinies. So the UK lost the opportunity of playing a leading role in shaping the new Europe.

The reorganized Europe was brought about by the efforts of six countries ('the Six'), these being France, West Germany, Italy, the Netherlands, Belgium and Luxembourg. Working together they created the European Coal and Steel Community (ECSC) in 1951 and the European Atomic Energy Community (Euratom) in 1957. Also in 1957 they signed the **Treaty of Rome**, establishing the **European Economic Community** (EEC) from 1 January 1958. In 1967 the executives of these three Communities were merged and the amalgamated whole was termed the **European Community** (EC).

Enlargement of the Community

Although the UK did not relish economic integration and the implied loss of sovereignty which this entailed, it did see much sense in cooperation in terms of free trade. Along with other countries having similar attitudes – the traditionally neutral countries – the UK tried to avoid the economic isolation which being outside the EC implied, by forming a free trade area. The **European Free Trade Area** (EFTA) came into being under the Stockholm convention, signed on 4 January 1960. Its signatories were the UK, Austria, Denmark, Norway, Portugal, Sweden and Switzerland; EFTA was confined to trade in manufactures.

By the early 1960s the British government had changed its attitude to the Community. The UK's relative decline as a world power and changing trading patterns convinced British politicians that membership of the Community was desirable. In 1961 Harold Macmillan, the Conservative Prime Minister, announced that the UK would apply to join. This was not a popular move, sentiment being fairly conveyed by the *Daily Mail* cartoon reproduced here. Complicated negotiations followed, but they failed after two years when the French President, General de Gaulle, expressed the opinion that Britain was not yet sufficiently European to be admitted. In a change of government, Labour came to power and in

Brig.-Gen. GULLY SQUARE-LEGG, M.C.C.
(President Empire Umpires' Club)

"They'll be wanting us to play French cricket next, dammit!"

1967 Prime Minister Harold Wilson announced a new membership application. By the end of the year General de Gaulle had again effectively vetoed UK membership by announcing that such an event would destroy the Community. However, in 1969 he resigned and the Six agreed to open negotiations with the UK, Denmark, Ireland and Norway. The first three subsequently became full members on 1 January 1973. Although Norwegian negotiations also succeeded, the Norwegian people rejected membership in a referendum.

Further enlargements of the Community added Greece in 1981 and Portugal and Spain in 1986. All three countries had emerged from dictatorships immediately before making their applications to join, and saw the Community as offering political stability as well as economic benefits. In 1990, following the collapse of Communism in east Europe, East Germany was reunited with West Germany. These various enlargements of the Community are a source of confusion to the unwary: obviously Community data refer to a different mix of countries over time. A useful, but unfortunately not universal, convention is to write EUR6, EUR9, EUR10, EUR12 and EUR12+ (the latter sign indicating the inclusion of the former East Germany) to indicate which version of the Community is being discussed. In this book most data relate to EUR12 even for years before 1986 – by the simple expedient of adding figures for the non-members to the Community data. At the time of writing (spring 1994) negotiations for the accession of Austria, Finland, Norway and Sweden are expected to result in the accession of these countries on 1 January 1995.

Objectives of the European Economic Community

These are best expressed by quoting in full Article 2 of the Treaty of Rome:

> 'It shall be the aim of the Community, by establishing a Common Market and progressively approximating the economic policies of Member States, to promote throughout the Community a harmonious development of economic activities, a continuous and balanced expansion, an increased stability, an accelerated raising of the standard of living and closer relations between its Member States.'

This Article makes it clear that a common market is expected to be of economic benefit to its members. It ends by looking towards 'closer relations between its Member States', implying that economic progress will lead towards some degree of political integration. This is consistent with the vision of Monnet mentioned earlier.

What is a common market?

The economic principles are to be discussed in the next chapter. For the moment a brief answer is that it is a group of countries which have no trade barriers between its members, but with a common agreed trade policy towards third countries.

Goods, services, labour and capital can circulate freely within and between members as the forces of free competition dictate.

Since one of the main functions of government is to intervene in the national economy, some coordination of such interventions is essential to prevent the distortion of competitive forces by different government policies operating in the member states. Clearly this coordination requires organizing and the Community has special Community-level institutions to do this.

Community institutions

There are four major bodies: the European Commission, the Council of Ministers, the European Parliament and the Court of Justice.

The **European Commission** is the civil service of the Community. It is the main initiator of policy proposals, which it drafts and then discusses with the Council of Ministers, Parliament and a variety of interested parties. When policies have been decided it sees to their implementation as **Directives, Decisions** and **Regulations**. All three types of outcome have the force of law throughout member states – *if they conflict with national legislation it is the Community law which must prevail.*

Directives take effect through national legislatures, which are required to produce their own laws along the prescribed policy lines;

that is, the resultant laws are tailored to suit different national circumstances. A **Decision** is binding upon a named person, company or state. **Regulations** are more general, applying in an identical fashion throughout the Community.

When a policy has been agreed by the Council of Ministers, the Commission organizes its execution, often with the aid of national civil services. Indeed most of the day-to-day implementation of policies is in the hands of national civil servants acting virtually as agents of the Community. The Commission is too small to do anything more than supervise in this field – far from being the vast 'Brussels bureaucracy' imagined by some nationalists it employs less than half the number of civil servants one would find in some of the larger UK ministries.

The Commission has 17 members appointed by member states, each in charge of a major policy area. The professional civil servants working under them are divided into 22 **Directorates-General** (DGs). These are similar to ministries in the UK. Some of the big ones of immediate interest to economists are DG IV – Competition, DG VI – Agriculture, and DG VII – Transport.

The **Council of Ministers** is not a fixed body of individuals: its composition depends on the policy in question. For example, if the topic is agriculture it is comprised of the Ministers of Agriculture from each member state, for transport policy the Ministers of Transport form the Council. All decisions are taken by the Council of Ministers. They receive proposals from the Commission, they may instruct the Commission to formulate a particular policy, they adopt and amend policies. As the Council is formed of national politicians it is to be expected that much political 'horse trading' takes place which may result in agreements involving unrelated issues despite the best efforts of the Commission.

The **European Council** is a special council of *heads of state or government* which meets twice a year. This council takes the fundamental decisions of principle which determine the nature and direction of Community activities.

The **European Parliament** is a directly elected body of 518 members sitting in Strasbourg. It is largely a consultative body, receiving and commenting on Commission proposals before they are adopted by the Council. The latter can pass laws even if the Parliament disagrees with them. However, the Parliament does have some budgetary power and in particular can reject the Community draft budget, which it did in 1985, forcing a new budget to be formulated. It can also, by a two-thirds majority, dismiss the Commission, though it would have no say in the appointment of replacements.

The **Court of Justice** is based in Luxembourg. It has 13 judges, including one from each member state. The Court's judgements are binding throughout the Community. Indeed member states or institutions can be taken to the Court by individuals, organisations, other institutions or other member states.

Decision-making and the Single European Act

The Treaty of Rome allowed for decisions to be reached by unanimous agreement during the early years of the Community. Later, with growing political and economic cohesion, decisions were to be reached through a system of qualified majority voting. In practice, member states were very reluctant to give up the power of veto which the unanimity rule implied. Getting the agreement of all member states was never easy and proved increasingly difficult as the Community was enlarged, so that policy initiatives necessary for the development of the Community were only agreed after protracted negotiations. By the early 1980s the Community seemed to be grinding to a halt.

Following much discussion in European Councils and the reports of special committees it was agreed to 'relaunch' the Community via a **Single European Act** (SEA) which was signed by all member states in February 1986. This Act is of great economic and political significance. It amended the Treaty of Rome in an attempt to achieve that Treaty's original economic objective of free trade within the Community. This was to be done by abolishing all internal barriers to trade, producing a **Single Market** by the end of 1992. Achievement of this boost to the Community economy was made possible by dropping the unanimity rule for decisions which did not involve points of principle. Thus decisions in the commercial field were now to be reached by qualified majority voting.

The qualified majority voting system gives ten votes each to France, Italy, Germany and the UK, eight to Spain, five each to Belgium, Greece, the Netherlands and Portugal, three each to Denmark and Ireland and two to Luxembourg. The total is 76, and 54 represents a qualified majority. The six largest votes add up to 53, so they cannot impose their views on the smaller countries.

The SEA also committed the Community to progress towards **Economic and monetary union** (EMU), and politically to include foreign policy and security. In 1990 a special committee was set up to study EMU and to make recommendations to the European Council planned for December 1991 in **Maastricht.** Meanwhile the collapse of the USSR power bloc led to the reunification of Germany. Although this took place in 1990 by East Germany being absorbed into the

Community, many were concerned that the enlarged Germany would become introspective and so hinder the further development of the Community. Chancellor Kohl of Germany and President Mitterand of France responded to such worries by proposing that EMU should be accompanied by political union. Accordingly another committee was set up to examine this, also to report to the European Council in Maastricht in 1991.

The Treaty of Maastricht

This was negotiated in the 1991 European Council. It further amended the Treaty of Rome and so had to be ratified by each of the twelve member states. Sovereignty implications were sufficiently controversial to make ratification by several members a slow and painful process. In the UK, the right wing of the ruling Conservative Party regarded the Treaty as highly undesirable and fought against it. Nevertheless, national ratifications completed, the Treaty came into force on 1 November 1993. Its three main features are:

- economic, social and political extensions to the existing EC
- common foreign and security policy
- intergovernmental cooperation on justice and home affairs.

The latter two aspects are outside the institutional framework of the Community. The net effect of the Treaty is to add a significant political dimension to the EC, the expanded whole forming the **European Union** (EU). This new title will be used in the remainder of this book except in historical contexts. The accompanying boxed article , reproduced from *The Economist*, discusses these momentous changes.

The EU budget

Unlike national budgets, the EU budget's only purpose is to finance common policies and administration. So it does not involve taxation, borrowing, deficits, the redistribution of incomes.

Initially, the budget had three sources of income:

- import duties
- agricultural import levies
- a VAT element.

Import duties and **levies** are collected at the point of entry regardless of the destination of the imports once within the EU. They are paid into the EU budget instead of accruing to the state of the port of origin but the latter keeps ten per cent to cover collection costs.

EU fugaces labuntur communitates*

FROM OUR BRUSSELS CORRESPONDENT

Just as most people had stopped talking about the 'common market' and become used to calling it the European Community, the Maastricht treaty comes along and confuses everyone by creating something called the European Union. What is it, and why has *The Economist* reluctantly decided to abandon the now familiar EC for the something-between-a-sigh-and-an-expletive EU?

The viscosity of the answer reflects that of the Maastricht treaty, which came into force on November 1st, bringing the Union with it. It is yet another masterpiece of Euro-fudge. The new Union is the old Community with two additions. One is a common foreign and security policy; the other is co-operation between the 12 governments in justice and police matters. The rest of what Maastricht is supposed to do – open the road to economic union and a single currency, strengthen the European Parliament, give Brussels new powers over industrial policy, consumer affairs, health and education – stays four-square with the EC.

The whole construction – EC plus foreign and security policy plus justice and police co-operation – adds up to the European Union. On the other hand, it does not add up to one single decision-taking process but to three separate ones. Moreover, the European Union has no legal persona. Only the EC, and/or the member-states, can conclude international agreements, for instance.

In other words, confusion reigns. It certainly does among the Union's architects. At a press conference after the recent Brussels summit, John Major fluffed his first attempt to explain what European Union is and why he would be using the name sparingly. He eventually spoke of a 'three-pillared union' within which the EC work would continue as before, while anything to do with foreign and security matters or justice and police would be strictly Union business. The main reason for this separation is the desire of several countries, led by Britain and France, to keep the Maastricht additions as much as possible out of the hands of the Brussels commission and the European Parliament. British officials in Brussels say they will try to maintain the distinction in day-to-day European affairs.

The Economist reckons that effort will be forlorn. Some people will go on talking about the Community regardless of legal accuracy, others will increasingly refer to the Union in all contexts except historical ones. We have decided to opt for the Union, believing (perhaps wrongly) that in time this term will prevail.

Source: *The Economist*, 20 Nov. 1993

*The latin word *eheu*, pronounced somewhat like EU, means 'alas'. This pun, from Horace, translates as, 'Alas, the fleeting communities slip by.'

Note that the **VAT element** is not an EU tax, it is only a basis for calculating member states' budgetary contributions. The Commission calculates the yield which a VAT on a uniform basis would provide if levied in each member country. So this element of the budget relates to a *notional* VAT. In 1970 the maximum rate of VAT was set at 1 per cent.

Budget problems and solutions

In 1984, spending on agriculture increased so much that the budget needed either to breach the VAT ceiling or to suspend payments. In the

Table 2 The EU's 1992 budget (million Ecu)

Expenditure		Revenue	
Agricultural support	32 579	Agricultural levies	2 209
Regional fund	8 571	Customs duties	12 548
Social fund	4 311	VAT own resource	34 595
Fisheries	410	GNP-based own resource	8 315
Administration	2 905	less collection costs	(1 477)
Other*	10 081	Other*	3 522
Total	58 857	Total	59 712

*Other expenditures include research and development, cooperation with non-member states, repayments to member states etc. Other revenues are balancing items from previous years, similar additions will appear in future years to balance this one.
Source: *Financial Report 1992,* Office for Official Publications, Luxembourg.

event it was saved by delaying some payments until the following year and by 'repayable advances' made by member states. The 1984 crisis persuaded the Council of Ministers to agree to curb agricultural spending and to raise the VAT ceiling to 1.4 per cent from 1986.

The budget was close to exhaustion in 1986 and 1987. In June 1988 it was agreed to add a fourth source of income (retrospectively from 1 January 1988). This is a **GNP-based contribution** from members. The total budgetary expenditure was limited to 1.15, 1.17, 1.18, 1.19 and 1.2 per cent of the EC's GNP in the years 1988 to 1992 respectively. In 1992 a further increase to a maximum of 1.27 per cent of EU GNP by 1999 was agreed. Table 2 outlines the main elements of the budget for 1992.

The significance of the GNP-based contribution is that it is more closely related to ability to pay than are the other budget revenues. In contrast agricultural and import levies depend on national patterns of imports, and the VAT contributions depend on national patterns of consumption. GNP-based contributions introduce the ability to pay principle for the first time, but there is no element of progressivity in the distribution of the tax burden.

Conclusion
The UK threw away its post-war opportunity to be a major force in the reshaping of Europe. Yet only three years after the Common Market began the UK was applying, unsuccessfully, to join. Subsequently the UK

and five other countries joined, and are now part of a process of increasing integration, the *'ever closer union'* called for in the Treaty of Rome.

KEY WORDS

Jean Monnet	European Council
Economic integration	European Parliament
Political union	Court of Justice
Treaty of Rome	Single European Act
European Economic	Single Market
Community (EEC)	Economic and monetary union
European Community (EC)	Maastricht
European Free Trade Area	European Union (EU)
(EFTA)	EU budget
European Commission	Import duties
Directives	Levies
Decisions	VAT element
Regulations	GNP-based contribution
Directorates-General	Fourth resource
Council of Ministers	

Essay topics

1. In what ways has economic integration already occurred in the European Community? Assess the economic issues involved in determining the future form of economic integration. (University of Cambridge Local Examinations Syndicate, 1993)
2. Examine the arguments for unrestricted international trade. In the light of these arguments, how could you justify the imposition of tariffs on US goods by the European Community? (University of London Examinations and Assessment Council, 1990)
3. How is Britain's contribution to the European Community budget determined? Is is reasonable to expect Britain to pay a larger contribution in future? (Oxford & Cambridge Schools Examination Board, 1993)

Data Response Question 1
The European Community budget
This task is based on a question set by the Oxford & Cambridge Schools Examination Board in 1992. Study Figure A and Table A, and answer the questions that follow. Note that the data in Figure A are in billions of Ecus, with 1 Ecu roughly equivalent to 70 pence.

1. Give brief explanations of the following: (i) agricultural levies; (ii) customs duties; (iii) VAT/financial contributions.
2. Why is Britain a net contributor to the EC budget?
3. What criticisms have been made of the large proportion of the budget devoted to agricultural price support (nearly £23 billions in 1991)? What action, if any, has been taken in response to these criticisms?

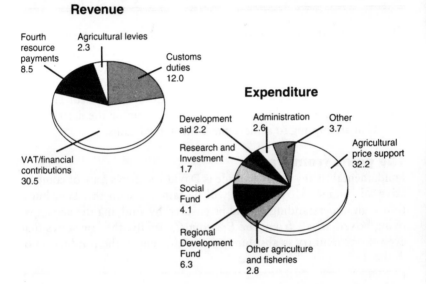

Figure A The 1991 EC budgeted revenue and expenditure

Table A UK contributions and receipts from the EC budget (£bn)

	1986	1987	1988	1989	1990	1991
UK gross contributions	4.5	5.2	5.1	5.6	6.4	6.3
UK receipts	2.2	2.3	2.2	2.1	2.2	2.8
Refund under						
Fontainebleu abatement*	1.7	1.2	1.6	1.1	1.7	2.4
Net contribution	0.6	1.7	1.3	2.3	2.5	1.1

*UK's *gross* contribution in any given year is reduced by an amount broadly equivalent to two-thirds of *net* contribution in the previous year.
Source: *Economic Briefing*, HM Treasury, May 1991.

Chapter Two

Economic integration

*'... the principle of comparative advantage ... is perhaps the most
powerful idea in economics...' The Economist*

This chapter attempts to answer the question – what are the economic
benefits of a common market? On the theoretical side the gains from
trade, due to the operation of comparative advantage, are analysed
and related to different levels of economic integration. Finally, the
expected size of gains to be achieved by the EU are discussed. This sets
the scene for the remaining chapters which examine the activities of
the EU in attempting to achieve these theoretical gains.

The gains from trade

Fundamental to any study of trade is David Ricardo's **Law of comparative advantage.** Most readers will be familiar with this law, but a
thorough understanding should be ensured by studying the accompanying boxed article from *The Economist*. Briefly, the law states that
even if one country is absolutely more efficient in the production of

---

How to make comparative advantage work for you

These days politicians all over the world
declare themselves in favour of *free
trade*. When it comes to voting for it,
they are not so sure. The reason is not
just the pressure of special-interest politics. It is also that most people have im-
bibed the prejudice that free trade is a
good thing, without imbibing the economics that ought to lie behind it. What
this prejudice says, in fact, is that free
trade is a good thing only if everybody
else joins in; one-sided, or unilateral,
free trade is a mug's game. The classical
case for free trade argues exactly the opposite: *free trade is good for a country
even if other countries do not return the
favour.*

Writing 40 years before Ricardo,
Adam Smith had already had a lot to say

about the gains from trade. He saw it as,
among other things, a way of promoting
efficiency, both because it fostered competition and because it provided opportunities to specialise and gain
economies of scale. Specialisation was a
matter of absolute advantage: trade allows countries to produce what they are
best at, and buy in the rest.

This view begged a question: what if
Britain, say, is bad at making
everything? Does this not mean that
trade would drive all its producers
out of business? David Ricardo
answered the question by formulating the principle of comparative
advantage. *This is perhaps the single
most powerful idea in
economics.*

Help yourself to wine and cheese.

Suppose there are two countries, Utopia and Flatland, and that these countries produce just two goods, wine and cheese. In Utopia it takes one hour of labour to make a pound of cheese and two hours to make a gallon of wine. In Flatland it takes six hours to make a pound of cheese and three hours to make a gallon of wine. Note that Utopia is more productive than Flatland in both goods; it has an absolute advantage in wine and cheese. But its greater advantage, its comparative advantage, is in cheese. This will determine what happens when the two countries trade.

The precise outcome will depend on the pattern of demand, and hence on the price of each good in terms of the other once trade begins. Assume that a pound of cheese trades for a gallon of wine. This is for simplicity's sake; the argument does not turn on the price chosen. In Utopia, which is better at making both goods, an hour of labour can make either a pound of cheese or a gallon of wine. But since a pound of cheese can be traded for a gallon of wine, it makes sense for Utopia to specialise in producing cheese, and then trade some of its cheese for wine. In this way it can consume as much cheese as before and twice as much wine, or some combination of more wine and cheese.

Flatland is less efficient than Utopia at making both goods. But in Flatland too it pays to specialise. An hour of its labour can make one-sixth of a pound of cheese or one-third of a gallon of wine (which is worth one-third of a pound of cheese in the international market). So Flatland specialises in the production of wine, and trades some of its wine for cheese. Trade means that it can consume as much wine as before and twice as much cheese, or some combination of more of both.

From the assumptions this example has already made, it is possible to deduce the market-determined wage that will be paid in each country. The hourly wage in Utopia will be a pound of cheese (equal to a gallon of wine) and the wage in Flatland will be one-third of a gallon of wine (equal to one-third of a pound of cheese). In other words, the wage in Utopia will be three times the wage in Flatland. This reflects the relative price of the two goods, together with the fact that Utopia is six times more productive in cheese and 1 1/2 times more productive in wine.

Here is another way to think of it. Utopia is more efficient overall, so its wages are higher. This give Flatland an opportunity to produce at lower cost, provided it specialises in wine, the good in which it has a comparative advantage (that is, a smaller absolute disadvantage). Utopia can make a gallon of wine with two hours of labour, whereas Flatland needs three – but because its wages are only one-third of Utopia's, Flatland can produce wine more cheaply. (Despite the fact that its wages are lower, Flatland cannot produce cheese more cheaply.)

Trade does not equalise incomes when productivity differs across countries, it just makes all sides better off than they would otherwise be. Moreover, trade always uncovers opportunities of this kind. Repeat, nothing central to the argument rests on the particular assumptions about price and productivity that have been used in this example.

The example has been borrowed, by the way, from an excellent textbook, *International Economics*, written by Messrs Paul Krugman (the very same) and Maurice Obstfeld. You will find it on page 22 – the principle of comparative advantage is not exactly advanced material. In parts of the real world, though, the free-trade debate still seems to be struggling with page xi (List of Contents). Krugman and Obstfeld quote with amusement an article from the *Wall Street Journal* ('The coming overthrow of free trade') which observed, 'Many small countries have no comparative advantage in anything.' One can imagine the writer prefacing that jewel of economic illiteracy with 'Of course, we all believe in free trade, but ...'

Source: *The Economist.* 22 Sept. 1990

every good than is some second country, if each country specializes in the production of the products in which it has a comparative advantage (i.e. greatest *relative* efficiency – it produces the goods it is *best* at producing), then trade will benefit both countries.

The benefits of trade due to comparative advantage are reinforced by **economies of size** (usually referred to incorrectly as economies of scale). This refers to the fact that, for many forms of production, average costs decline as output is expanded, at least until very large outputs are achieved. Specialization according to comparative advantage means that firms will have larger markets and will be enabled to grow larger, and hence have lower costs. This is a **dynamic process**, for large firms with low costs and high profits are able to invest in expensive research and development, *which enables these firms' productivity to continue to improve.* In fields of production involving complex modern technology, only very large firms can afford to keep abreast of new developments and so compete successfully in world markets.

The most obvious gain from trade is the increased choice of goods for customers. If the UK had to be self-sufficient – unable for some reason to trade with other countries – the range of goods available would be greatly diminished. For example, it is possible to produce bananas in a hothouse, but only at such high cost that few would be able to buy them. If your breakfast today included cornflakes, and tea or coffee, what would you have had instead of these imported products?

Completely free trade benefits all participants, so why then is trade restricted by **tariffs** and other measures? There are four basic reasons:

- ignorance
- selfishness
- health
- strategic arguments.

Ignorance of the real economic facts is possible because decisions are not taken by economists but by politicians – often on the basis of a wide variety of fallacious economic arguments.

More likely is *selfishness*. Imagine that a major employer in your locality is suffering competition from imported goods and is consequently soon to become bankrupt. The local Member of Parliament persuades the government to intervene by assisting the uncompetitive firm. What assistance is likely? A subsidy would underline the firm's uncompetitive situation and so be inadvisable, but a tariff on imports would reduce or remove the imports (often described as 'unfair' competition) and raise prices, thus returning the firm to profitability and ensuring the jobs of its employees. But such a tariff is little different from a subsidy in that it enables an uncompetitive firm to survive. A major difference is that a subsidy is paid for by taxpayers, making it obvious and unacceptable, whilst a tariff is paid for by consumers through higher prices (and reduced supplies) which seem to go unnoticed. Clearly a tariff benefits a minority at the expense of society in general. Those about to go bankrupt or lose their jobs are vociferous, whilst consumers are more dispersed and unorganized and so make no effective complaint. Consequently protective tariffs are exceedingly common.

The third reason for trade barriers is to protect *public health*. Such trade restrictions are intended to ensure that imported canned products, for example, meet reasonable health standards, and clearly *some* measures of this type are justified.

Finally, *strategic* reasons for protective tariffs or subsidies refer to a country's need to safeguard its food supply, and manufacturing industries capable of producing guns, aircraft and ships in case of war; this is clearly not an *economic* justification.

Effects of tariff removal in a customs union

Referring to Figure 1, P_1 is the initial price in say the UK, domestic supply is Q_{S1} and consumption Q_{D1}. As a result of the removal of an import tariff after joining the customs union the price falls to P_2 and consumption rises to Q_{D2} whilst domestically produced supply falls to Q_{S2}. Clearly consumers are better off because they now consume more of the good at a lower price. The resources which had been devoted to producing $Q_{S1} - Q_{S2}$ are released for the production of other goods. Imports have increased from M_1 to M_2, the extra coming from another member or other members of the customs union where there is a comparative advantage in the production of this good. Similarly, for some other good for which the UK has a comparative advantage, tariff

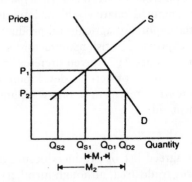

Figure 1 The consequences of a price reduction

17

removal in other member states will provide the UK with an expanded market and the production of this other good will employ the resources released by the contraction of production of the first good. **Trade creation** is the term given to such cases; clearly it benefits all members of the customs union.

Trade diversion is a potential disadvantage of joining a customs union. Remember that when the tariffs on trade between members are removed, they are replaced by common tariffs between the group and the rest of the world. So the common external tariff may mean that a country buys a particular good from its fellow members although it previously imported it more cheaply from a third country. It is intuitively obvious that, provided that the common external tariff adopted is not higher on average than the previous tariffs of member states which it replaces, the gains from trade creation will exceed the losses from trade diversion.

This analysis has been conducted in terms of tariffs. Clearly the gains from tariff removal are applicable to the removal of any other forms of trade barriers.

Economic integration

There are five levels of economic integration between countries. *Inevitably each implies a degree of political integration which could be regarded as some pooling of sovereignty.*

Preference areas

These are agreements to give privileged access to certain products from specified countries. Thus, following the Ottawa Conference of 1932, a system of Imperial Preference was introduced for trade between the UK and countries of the British Empire. This involved a **reciprocal reduction** of tariffs on trade between the participants, although tariffs against outsiders remained relatively high. Imperial Preference was designed to help the exports of agricultural products from the Empire to Britain, and the exports of British manufacturers to the Empire. The **Lomé convention** has since 1975 given preferential access to the EU market for some products of certain developing countries. In this instance the preferential treatment is one-way, and is regarded as a form of development aid.

Free trade areas

Here, trade in an agreed list of products occurs freely between the members of the free trade area, although members retain their independent tariffs against third countries. *Such an arrangement is an*

AT THE CROSS-ROAD

attempt to gain the benefits of comparative advantage and specialization with a minimal loss of sovereignty. The political content of an agreement is limited to rules which are necessary for its fair operation. The European Free Trade Area which the UK joined in 1960 is a good example (see Chapter 1).

Customs union

This extends the free trade area idea to include a **common external tariff** against third countries. However, it involves far more political cooperation than does a free trade area. For example, the member states have to agree on the levels of tariff set and on their revision. This will obviously involve joint trade negotiations with third countries.

Common market

This adds *freedom of movement for factors of production* (labour and capital) to the free trade in goods and services of a customs union. Proper application of the law of comparative advantage requires that there are no distortions to competition. Consequently much common policy formulation is required and so a great deal of political cooperation is essential.

Economic and monetary union

A common market between member states having separate currencies still involves some internal trade barriers. These are **transactions costs** and **uncertainty**. The former relate to the cost of buying and selling currencies which are obviously part of any trade in goods and services. Uncertainty arises because exchange rates can alter between the time when a deal is planned and the time when it is executed, and such a change may turn profit into loss. The full exploitation of comparative advantage is only possible if there is a single currency. Thus economic and monetary union describes the situation when two or more countries unite their economies completely. *In turn this implies political union also*, for the effective control of an economy covers the money supply, taxation, the redistribution of incomes – in short, all the major economic decisions undertaken by a modern state.

Expected economic benefits of the EU

As discussed in the previous chapter, the removal of tariff barriers is a necessary but not sufficient condition for free trade. The EU failed to follow up its initial removal of tariffs on internal trade with the

The Single European Act

In December 1985, the European Council (the Heads of State or Government) meeting in Luxembourg, decided to give new impetus to European integration by drawing up a 'Single European Act', which was signed in February 1986 and came into force on 1 July 1987.

The Single Act is a new Treaty which modifies and supplements the Treaties of Paris and Rome (which established the three European Communities: ECSC, EEC, Euratom). Its aim is to bring the Community into line with the needs of the 1990s and to shape it into one large economic unit, a truly frontier-less internal market with a population of 320 million: the biggest in the world.

Acting on the fact that Europe's lack of integration is proving expensive to the citizens of the Community (costing between ECU 125 and 190 thousand million per year according to studies carried out by the Commission), the decision-makers in the Member States have decided to do everything possible to create, by 1 January 1993, a 'vast single market'. Citizens of the Twelve will be able to live and work in the country of their choice, regardless of what job they do. Tourists and travellers will be able to travel without frontier checks and use their credit cards in all the countries of the Community. Businesses will have a far wider market, leading to greater profitability from investment and the creation of employment – in short, an area in which there will be total freedom of movement for persons, goods and capital.

Source: *Europe in Figures*, 1989/90 edn, Eurostat

required complementary measures, and so after an initial decade of rapid growth, relative stagnation set in. The **Single European Act** was passed in 1986 to remedy this situation. It aimed at the removal of *all* trade barriers by the end of 1992 in a programme which is discussed in the next chapter.

As the accompanying boxed article from *Europe in Figures* indicates, the Single European Market was estimated to make the EU better off to the tune of Ecu125 milliard to Ecu190 milliard (£84 billion to £127 billion) per year. Such figures are difficult to comprehend, but percentages give a sense of perspective: according to the Commission, EU GDP was estimated to increase by about 4.5 per cent and employment by 1.5 per cent whilst inflation would be slightly reduced. These are 'static benefits' – those that should be achieved within the first few years. In the long term the **dynamic benefit** was an expected increase of about one percentage point in the rate of economic growth.

Conclusion

This chapter has concentrated on the theoretical gains from comparative advantage. The gains *expected* turn out to be impressively large, but *how* has the EU attempted to capture them, and are the gains *equitably distributed?* We now turn to these questions in the next few chapters.

KEY WORDS	
Law of comparative advantage	Reciprocal reduction
Economies of size	Lomé convention
Dynamic process	Common external tariff
Tariffs	Transactions costs
Trade creation	Uncertainty
Trade diversion	Single European Act
Economic integration	Static benefits
	Dynamic benefit

Reading list

Anderton, A., Units 84 and 85 in *Economics,* Causeway Press, 1991.
Smith, C., Chapter 2 in *UK Trade and Sterling*, 2nd edn, Heinemann Educational, 1994.

Essay topics

1. Distinguish between the principles of absolute advantage and comparative advantage. Explain how the principles can be applied to determine the gains made from international trade, both in theory and practice. (University of Cambridge Local Examinations Syndicate, AS Level, 1991)
2. What are the benefits of international trade? Discuss whether or not the formation of trading blocs such as the European Community contributes to an increase in economic welfare. (Associated Examining Board, 1993)
3. Discuss the advantages and disadvantages of specialization for: (a) a worker, (b) a firm, (c) a country. (University of Oxford Delegacy of Local Examinations, 1992)
4. The principle of comparative advantage suggests that society benefits from specialization and free trade. (a) Explain the principle of comparative advantage, outlining the benefits which are likely to result from free trade. (b) Evaluate three different arguments for the imposition of restrictions upon international trade. (Associated Examining Board, 1994)
5. Outline the economic advantages and disadvantages of a customs union. Explain how the European Community's external trade policy has sought to reduce these disadvantages. (Joint paper, Oxford & Cambridge SEB/Cambridge LES, AS Level, 1992)

Data Response Question 2

Levies versus free trade

This task is based on a question set by the University of Cambridge Schools Examination Board in 1990.

In 1988 the European Community imposed a special levy on the import of Japanese dot matrix printers, amounting to 33.4 per cent. This spurred the Japanese manufacturers into public outrage. On 8 September 1988, one of the leading manufacturers, Epson, published a large advertisement in national newspapers, the text of which is reproduced here. Read the Epson case, and then answer the questions that follow.

'We acted like any good business should'

On May 27th, 1988, the members of a special Commission investigating claims by European printer manufacturers into alleged Japanese 'dumping' delivered their verdict.

Guilty.

The price to be paid? A stiff levy on Japanese dot matrix printers.

That includes us, Epson. The world's leading producers of printers and, facing a levy of 33.4%, now a rather bemused spokesman for the Japanese printer industry.

Maybe you think Japan deserves levies. Or maybe the whole thing seems irrelevant to you.

If so, it may surprise you to know that 67% of the UK business community polled by MORI (Market & Opinion Research International) were against the imposition of levies recognising that it would increase their costs.

What's at stake here should deeply concern you if you believe there's any kind of relationship between Free Trade and successful business.

It's our opinion that the levy is unjust. It's been arrived at on the basis of calculations, statistics and reasoning which are demonstrably wrong.

But what's worse for all of us in business, whether in the East or the West, is that the levy is counter productive.

It may well harm the very industry it's designed to protect. And if it breeds more legislation like it, you may find you rue the day you missed your chance to prevent it spreading no matter what business you're in.

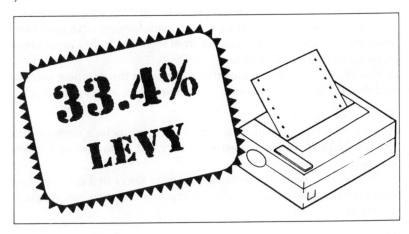

Again, these are things you might expect us to say. But we're not objecting to this levy just so that we can be seen to put up some kind of fight.

We are fundamentally opposed to it and, with respect, would ask you to listen to our case.

An unfair comparison

Most Japanese companies (ourselves included) make healthy profits on their overseas trade – not something you achieve by selling below cost.

So the Commission had to look elsewhere for this elusive proof of dumping.

They looked at the price Japanese printers are sold for to dealers in Japan and compared this with the price dealers in Europe buy them for.

But this was not a 'like for like' comparison.

All of Epson's European costs, right down to postage stamps, were deducted, whereas in Japan only marketing and selling costs were considered.

Small wonder they found a discrepancy ...

A different market

Equally, in its deliberations, the Commission compared European and Japanese manufacturers as if we were all competing for the same marlet.

This is patently not so.

Europe chose several years ago to concentrate on the niche market of high price, heavy duty printers.

Japan (and Epson in particular) chose to develop the high volume, IBM compatible market in Europe.

Quite freely and independently, we both went out separate ways.

It seems absurd to us that European manufacturers can now complain that we are stealing a market from then which they never chose to be a part of in the first place.

And the Commission tell us that to decrease the dumping margin, and thus the levy, all we have to do is increase our prices in Europe!

Where will it all end?

There's even talk now of extending the levy to include components, not just finished products, apparently to punish us for having brought manufacturing jobs to Europe.

Ironically, if our manufacturing base were Korea or Taiwan and we imported our printers, to sell them at much lower prices, we would be unaffected.

The European Commission talks about Japanese manufacturing plants destroying jobs in Europe. But these are jobs Europe never had. The new jobs created have in fact been transferred directly from Japan.

Isn't that what the Commission wanted?

The fact remains, because we have invested in Europe, we are to be penalised.

This in the face of our open commitment to finding components within Europe whenever possible.

These things can't happen overnight.

Our products sell on quality and reliability. Given a reasonable amount of time, we will find that quality in Europe and gladly incorporate it into our products.

At the moment the duty of 33.4% is only provisional. But it's due to be made more definite in November.

We think it penalises us unfairly for being an astute, successful business. We also agree with those who call it 'a tax on users'.

If we are to make Free Trade something more than a slogan in the European Market, we should join in exposing the levy for what it really is, a "measure so transparently inept that it might just help to discredit Europe's fondness for self-destructive trade policy" (The Economist 4/6/88).

1. Explain what is meant by 'dumping'.
2. (a) What evidence was used by the European Community to determine that the Seiko Epson Corporation was dumping its products in the European market?
   (b) On what grounds did the Seiko Epson Corporation reject this evidence?
3. What are the likely effects of the 33.4 per cent levy on each of the following? (i) UK business consumers. (ii) The Seiko Epson Corporation's manufacturing operations in Europe. (iii) The operations of other Japan-based manufacturers of printers.
4. In the light of this particular case, evaluate the arguments for and against import levies.

Chapter Three
The Single Market

Non tariff barriers are effective trade barriers. Before the Single European Act it would have taken an accountant 50 years to qualify and requalify in each member country so as to be able to audit in each country!

This chapter examines how free competition within the EU – the Single Market – can be achieved; it involves removing many other impediments as well as tariffs on internal trade before goods and services can flow freely. The Single Market also has significant social implications which are noted here. Finally, as trade with the rest of the world is more important to the EU than to any other major bloc or country, it is appropriate to discuss the attitude to competition in world markets.

Internal competition
It should be remembered that a common market involves the free movement of goods, services, capital and labour between a group of countries. Emphasis is to be laid on the word *free*, both here and in the term 'free competition'. *Only in a free market can comparative advantage, specialization and concomitant economies of size be attained.*

Economies of size in many fields of industrial production can be gained only by very large firms, much larger than those existing within the EU when it was formed. This implies either the growth of some firms, and the demise of their internal competitors, or their growth by merger and acquisition regardless of member state boundaries. Unfortunately the arrival of 'European firms' large enough to compete successfully in world markets with the largest American and Japanese firms requires the removal of national legal, technical and fiscal barriers by **harmonization** (an important EU concept which has sometimes threatened curious anomalies), *implying the replacement of national by Union-wide laws, standards and taxes.*

Harmonization in the industrial field has turned out to be extremely slow and difficult – this was one of the factors behind the introduction of the Single European Act (SEA) already mentioned, and discussed in detail below. The only significant industrial activity undertaken at Community level before the SEA was its assistance to declining industries, steel being the major example. The European steel industry suffered from chronic excess capacity and lack of international competitiveness. Its reduction in size and its modernization were coordinated by the EU, greatly assisted by the existence of the European Coal and Steel Community, which provided the necessary mechanisms.

Removing tariffs on internal trade is a necessary but not sufficient condition for free internal trade. A plethora of **non-tariff barriers** (NTBs) and state aids can effectively prevent or greatly reduce trade. NTBs include different technical standards and complex documentation. Before the Single Market, the manufacturer of a product might have to produce it in twelve different versions to satisfy different national criteria, and similarly provide different documentation for each member state, involving several languages. There are many other ways in which internal trade may be distorted, and the one which attracts most attention is *state aid*. Helping industries through the provision of production subsidies, artificially low interest rates, research and development expenditures, and so on, may be legitimate (though economically dubious) government activities, but if practised differently by the individual member states competition will obviously be distorted.

Competition policy

The discussion so far has focused on national government policies, but private firms can also indulge in practices which distort **competition**. Price fixing and market sharing cartels are the prime examples. Indeed, the initiation of the 1992 Programme (see p. 29) encouraged such a rash of mergers and acquisitions across national frontiers that some analysts asked if these were to capture the benefits of large-scale production or represented the cartelization of Europe.

National governments have long had their own measures to combat cartels. The Community leaves the control of cartels within member states to the members themselves unless there is an appreciable effect on trade between members. In the latter case *the Commission has wide powers to prohibit agreements intended to prevent, restrict or distort competition within the Single Market.*

Similarly, the Commission can prevent a firm which has a '**dominant position**' (e.g. a monopoly) from abusing that position. Note that having a dominant position *is* permitted – indeed the Community wishes to see more very large European firms capable of competing with the largest foreign firms in the world market. It is only the *abuse* of dominance which is prohibited.

Control over mergers and acquisitions which might give rise to a dominant position was agreed in 1989 along the following lines. Any

A textbook cartel that broke all the rules

For months, Europe's unsubsidised steel makers have denounced the underhand way some governments finance their weaker brethren. Now they themselves have been found guilty of dirty tricks. On February 16th, in what he dubbed "a textbook cartel case that broke every rule,' Karel Van Miert, the European Union's competition commissioner, announced record fines totalling 104m ecus ($117m) against 16 companies for rigging the market in steel beams.

The ringleaders in the cartel included British Steel (which was fined 32m ecus), and Unimetal, part of France's Usinor Sacilor group (12.3m ecus). According to Mr Van Miert, the steel makers used their cosy Brussels club, Eurofer, to put the cartel together virtually under the noses of his trust-busters. The steelmen also spun a web of bilateral deals among themselves, agreeing upon prices, staying out of each other's markets and exchanging confidential commercial information. The commission can fine firms up to 10% of their turnover in the market affected. The figure for British Steel was the equivalent of 7%, one of the highest rates ever imposed.

Source: *The Economist*, 19 Feb. 1994

firms whose desired merger seems likely to meet the regulation's criteria must notify the Commission of their proposals. The Commission will decide within one month whether to start proceedings and will then have four months in which to reach a final decision. Satisfying three criteria will cause the Commission to act:

- Merging firms have a combined world turnover exceeding 5 billion Ecu (£3.6bn).
- At least 250 million Ecu of turnover is generated within the EU.
- Less than two-thirds of the combined turnover comes from one member state.

The last criterion means that mergers with no major EU dimension remain the responsibility of national authorities such as the UK's Monopolies and Mergers Commission.

The EU Commission vets proposed mergers against the concept of a dominant position which significantly impedes effective competition. The regulation deals with any form of concentration of economic power and thus may include partial mergers and some joint ventures.

This regulation is to be reviewed in 1994. The Commission is likely to propose that its powers should be extended to mergers involving over 2 billion Ecu, and is expected to be strongly opposed by the UK. The accompanying box gives an example of the policy in action in an extract from *The Economist*.

The Single European Act and 1992 Programme

In Chapter 1, the SEA was described as the 'relaunching' of the Community. It was necessitated by the effect of non-tariff barriers, preventing the free movement of goods, services, capital and labour within the Community, and the slow progress made towards the removal of these barriers under the unanimity system of decision making. In 1985 the European Council agreed to this Act to remove NTBs and create a single European market by the end of 1992.

The SEA amended the Treaty of Rome, and came into force on 1 July 1987. Since then NTBs have been progressively removed over a wide field, decisions being greatly speeded by the adoption of a system of majority voting (see Chapter 1).

Purchasing by governments and other public bodies accounts for about 15 per cent of the EU's GDP. Traditionally such purchases have been almost exclusively from national suppliers and contractors. As part of the **1992 Programme,** such **public procurement** has been the subject of new directives which aim to ensure that all companies in the EU have a fair chance of tendering for such contracts regardless of national frontiers. These directives prohibit discriminatory specifications and complex tendering procedures, and force major contracts to be advertised at EU level with reasonable time limits for bids to be received. Purchasers must be prepared to justify their rejection of bids, and complaints can be taken to the Court of Justice.

Electricity generating equipment and railway equipment are typical of the sectors most affected by these rules. Traditionally each national public authority favoured its national champions, with the consequence that intra-EU trade in such products was very small, price differences between member states were substantial, and rates of capacity utilization were low. Clearly, because the potential economies of size in these sectors are very great, *the Single Market rules will lead to a major restructuring through mergers, concentration, and closure of plants.*

In the long term the EU aims to harmonize business laws and technical standards, but this is a very slow process. In the short term some pragmatic changes have been introduced to free markets from legal and technical NTBs. Thus, a standard **Single European Document** has been introduced to accompany goods being sent across national frontiers, replacing a plethora of complex national documents.

Most important on the technical front is the principle that what is acceptable in one member state must be acceptable in others. For example, in Germany, regulations insist that beer must be made from water, malt and hops only; all other additives are prohibited, and so Germany refused to permit beer imports from other member states. The Court of Justice ruled that notwithstanding their national rules, the Germans must permit the import of beers from other members –

additives and all – provided that such beers meet with the national standards in their countries of origin. This principle of **mutual recognition** is the key which has unlocked the door to the free movement of goods long before European standards can be agreed.

Financial services is one of the most rapidly growing sectors of the European economies, but cross-frontier competition was prevented by NTBs. Consequently this sector was targeted in the 1992 Programme, and its liberalization was expected to contribute one-third of all the economic gains from the introduction of the Single Market. Two factors explain the lack of competition in financial services:

- Cross-frontier competition was impossible so long as national governments maintained capital exchange controls.
- Each government had its own regulatory framework.

Regulation in this sector is essential, to control the money supply, for example, and to protect bank depositors from fraud.

The Treaty of Rome called for the free movement of goods, labour and *capital*, but little was done to promote freedom for capital because of the autonomy of national monetary authorities and potential or actual balance of payments problems. However, under the 1992 Programme, a 1988 directive was agreed which freed capital movements for eight countries, to be followed in 1992 by Spain and Ireland. Balance of payments difficulties were expected to delay the removal of controls by Greece and Portugal for a further three years.

In 1989 three directives were agreed to liberalize the banking sector. The new EU regulatory framework is based on mutual recognition and **subsidiarity** (see definition p. 33). Although there are no new EU-level powers, it must be noted that the Maastricht Treaty looks towards the future creation of a **European Central Bank**, which of course would have wide regulatory powers (discussed in Chapter 6)

The gradual liberalization of intra-EU trade has brought about very large increases in trade between member countries. Table 3 provides the data to support this claim.

Tax harmonization

Article 99 of the Treaty of Rome called for the harmonization of indirect taxation, but the only major progress in this direction has been the adoption of VAT (based on the previous French system) as the *method* of collection. *The harmonization of rates of tax and excise duty is proving to be a particularly intractable problem, although members have committed themselves to this in principle as one of the provisions*

Table 3 EU member states' trade with other members as a percentage of their total trade in 1958 and 1992

| | Imports | | Exports | |
	1958	1992	1958	1992
Belgium/Luxembourg	56	71	55	75
Denmark	60	55	59	54
Germany*	36	55	38	54
Greece	54	63	51	64
Spain	32	60	47	66
France	28	66	31	63
Ireland	69	72	82	74
Italy	30	59	35	58
Netherlands	50	59	58	75
Portugal	53	74	39	75
United Kingdom	22	51	22	56
Total EUR12	35	59	37	61

*1958 = West Germany, 1992 = unified Germany.
Source: *European Economy, 55,* 1993.

of the Single European Act. Progress is hindered by the fact that all fiscal decisions are still subject to unanimity in the Council of Ministers.

Differences in VAT rates are considerable and, through their effect on market prices, clearly distort competition. Rates of excise duties (on alcohol, tobacco and fuel) vary even more.

Different VAT and excise duty rates have resulted in member states having to maintain border formalities to collect taxes on imports and refund them on exports on intra-EU trade. Clearly this makes nonsense of the Single Market for many goods. In 1994 border formalities are being replaced by other bureaucratic procedures, which may speed trade movements but still leave the distortions.

An obvious distortion is differences in excise duties on fuels, which result in very different transport costs. The boxed extract overleaf, from the Nottingham *Evening Post*, takes a humerous look at the consequences of huge differences in member states' alcohol excise duties in the first year of the Single Market.

Social aspects of competition
Initially, social policy concentrated on retraining workers who became unemployed in the 1960s as a result of structural changes during this early period of rapid economic growth. More recently the **European Social Fund** has become one of the structural funds which are intended

Get loaded on 'Booze Cruise'

C'est formidable. The French have finally revealed how much beer they sold the British this year – nearly 16 pints for every person of drinking age.

A year after cross-Channel trade barriers came down and the British began going to France en masse for cheap drink, the figures prove conclusively that Brits like their beer as much as the French like their wine. Especially at those prices.

Victory

The trend also poses a growing threat to the traditional British pub and off-licence, both of which are starting to feel the pinch now that one pint in every eight drunk at home is imported – legally or illegally – from France.

It is hard to say who can claim victory in the latterday Norman Conquest that has seen 120,000 Britons crossing the Channel each week from Dover to Calais.

It is certainly a mutually beneficial arrangement. The French hypermarkets rake in the cash from British beer buyers and the ferry companies are making a packet from the booming cross-Channel 'Booze Cruise', which transports 18 tons of beer back to Britain every day.

The drinkers have been saving a fortune in duty, while profiteers can cash in further by selling beer illegally at a profit back home – thanks to the law that allows unlimited amounts of beer to be brought over for 'personal use'.

How can Customs prove you are not buying a year's supply? The only definite losers are the Government, who charge 30p per pint in duty, compared with 4p in France.

The UK – Europe's second-cheapest producer of beer after Portugal – now charges the second highest rate of duty after Ireland, with one-third of the cost of every pint going to the Exchequer in duty and VAT.

So much beer is being brought in from France that no one can produce accurate figures. But wildly differing figures from each side of the Channel are both far higher than all pre-Christmas estimates.

The chamber of commerce in Calais estimates that 500 million litres of beer, wine and spirits have been sold so far this year, of which up to 80 per cent is beer. In English pub measures, that's 712 million pints.

The Brewers' Society estimates that a more conservative 150 million litres of beer – a mere 263 million pints – will have come in from France alone during 1993.

Output

But that is still more than the annual output of a British brewery like Youngs and Fullers, and the loss in excise duty to the Government will be around £240 million. With wine and spirits, the figure doubles to almost £500 million.

Brewers' Society spokesman Mike Ripley said: 'The problem is that we just pay too much tax on booze here.

'We are not just out of line with the rest of Europe, we are way out of line. And as long as there is that incentive, you will have people going abroad to buy it more cheaply'.

Source: *Nottingham Evening Post*, 1 Jan. 1994

to help to redistribute more equitably the gains from freer competition; this aspect of social policy is discussed as part of regional policy in Chapter 5. In the current chapter we are concerned with distortions of competition which may arise as a result of differing national social conditions, and rights of workers.

The Commission felt that the introduction of the Single Market, with its stimulation of business, should be balanced by the development of social conditions which would ensure that all citizens would benefit. The economic programme was to be given a 'human face'. Accordingly, the **Social Charter** was produced, its first draft appearing in May 1989. It was discussed in June of that year by the Economic & Social Affairs Committee, and in December by the European Council. *It was broadly welcomed by eleven member states but opposed by the UK.* The Council made the following three points:

- In the construction of the Single Market, social aspects should be accorded the same importance as economic aspects.
- In the creation of the Single Market, job creation was to be given top priority.
- Implementation should comply with the principle of 'subsidiarity'.

The UK seized upon the term subsidiarity and took it to heart, claiming that the whole topic was best dealt with individually by member states.

The box on page 34 lists the 'fundamental rights' detailed in the Social Charter, *not all of which exist in the UK.* For example, there is no statutory right to annual paid leave in the UK, although this

---

The principle of subsidiarity

This principle became politically important when it was introduced in the Social Chapter of 1989 and emphasized in Article 3B of the Treaty of Maastricht. *Subsidiarity means that action should only be taken at European level when this offers a better way of achieving an objective than leaving it to member states.* In general terms, actions should be taken at the lowest possible level of government. Whilst the UK government has strongly supported this principle in so far as it affects its own relations with the EU, it usually ignores the principle in its dealings with local government within the UK.

The Charter of fundamental social rights for workers

The Charter features twelve rights:

- Freedom of movement of workers within the Community
- 'Fair' remuneration, protection to part-time workers
- Improved working conditions, including minimum annual paid leave and a weekly break from work
- Workers and unemployed to receive adequate social protection and social security payments
- Freedom of association and collective bargaining, including the right to choose whether or not to belong to a trade union and the right to strike
- Workers should be able to train and retrain throughout their working lives
- Equal treatment for men and women
- Workers should have rights relating to information, consultation and participation, particularly at times of restructuring, redundancies or the introduction of new technology
- Health and safety at work
- Protection of children and young people: this involves a minimum employment age, maximum hours of work, entitlement to vocational training after compulsory education
- Decent standard of living on retirement
- All disabled people should have additional help towards social and professional integration.

The Social Chapter

This is a protocol to the Maastricht Treaty accepted by all but the UK and so, like the Charter above, is *not* part of EU law. It is administered by the Commission and Council of Ministers without UK participation. In this unique situation new regulations can be introduced which will apply to all member states other than the UK.

The Chapter sets out an agenda for future progress and harmonization in:

- working conditions
- health and safety at work
- workers' rights to information and consultation
- removal of sexual discrimination in employment
- integration of differently abled people to the labour market
- social security

right already existed in all other members except Italy. Similarly, only the UK and Denmark did not impose a limit on working hours (as the publicity given to the hours worked by junior hospital doctors may remind us). There is no statutory right to strike in the UK, and works councils are not compulsory.

The social concerns of the other eleven members produced a follow-up to the Charter. They attempted to get its main provisions included in the Maastricht Treaty. Once again the UK refused and the outcome was a protocol to the Treaty.

Why was (and is) the UK government so opposed to these social aspects of the EU? *It claims that implementation of the implied social policies would raise costs of production and make Europe uncompetitive.* In support of these claims it notes that foreign countries' investment in Europe is being concentrated in the UK because of its refusal to adopt the EU's social aspirations. This is tantamount to admitting that the UK's attitude is causing distortion to fair competition! Further disputes over this subject cannot be far away.

External trade

The EU accounts for about 17 per cent of world trade and is the world's largest trading group. As Table 4 shows, EU exports to the world market far exceed those of the USA and Japan. External trade is about 10 per cent of Community GDP. Clearly no discussion of EU competition policy is complete without some consideration of the EU's position in world markets.

In 1947, the leading trading nations signed the **General Agreement on Tariffs and Trade** (GATT). This sought to avoid the protectionism

Table 4 Relative importance of EU in world trade, 1991 (milliard Ecu)

	Imports	Exports
EUR12+	494	424
USA	393	340
Japan	191	254
World	2836	2749
EUR12+ internal trade	706	693

Note: Surely world imports should equal world exports? Not exactly! First, data collection is not perfect; and second, exports travel for some time before becoming imports.
Sources: *Eurostatistics*, 1993; *UN Monthly Bulletin of Statistics*, 1993.

of the 1930s which had greatly exacerbated the worldwide 'Great Depression'. Its main aim was to reduce trade barriers, though it excluded agriculture and services. Its crucial principle is the **most-favoured nation** clause; under this, a country agreeing a tariff reduction to one country is obliged to offer the same reduction to all GATT members. How can the EU countries with zero internal tariffs and a common external tariff against third countries belong to GATT? The latter's rules exempt customs unions and free trade areas from this non-discrimination rule *provided that their formation does not raise the tariffs of the new trade group to a level greater on average than the previous tariffs of the individual members*. It is also permissible to offer reduced tariffs on a discriminatory basis to developing countries.

In Article 110 of the Treaty of Rome, the Community states its intention of contributing to

> '*the harmonious development of world trade, the progressive abolition of restrictions on international exchanges and the lowering of customs barriers*'.

To date the Community has two main discriminatory agreements: one is for reciprocal free trade in industrial products with the European Free Trade Area; the other – the Lomé convention – offers non-reciprocal tariff preferences for most non-agricultural goods and preferential access for some food products. The Lomé convention covers 66 African, Caribbean and Pacific (ACP) countries, mostly the ex-colonies of EU members. In addition to trade preferences it also provides aid for the ACP countries with special funds to stabilize their export earnings, and a European Development Fund to finance development projects.

From time to time GATT members enter a round of international negotiations to try to liberalize trade. As the EU has a common trade policy the Commission represents it, though its agreements have to be ratified by the Council of Ministers.

Successive rounds of negotiations in GATT since 1947 give the impression that trade barriers have been progressively reduced since tariffs have certainly fallen to low levels. *The truth is that their place was taken by NTBs*. Two examples underline the point. The Multi-fibre Arrangements (between developed-country textile importers, notably EU, USA and Japan, and developing-country exporters) placed quantitative restrictions on trade. Similarly, the EU's large trade deficit with Japan led to the imposition of Voluntary Export Restraints (VERs) on a wide range of goods such as motor cars and electronic items. Such quantitative restrictions became common.

In 1985 it was agreed to launch a new round of trade negotiations, the **Uruguay Round** (since this is where the initial conference was held), to be completed by the end of 1990. As this round was to include agriculture in addition to tariffs and NTBs, it is not surprising that progress was slow. The main protagonists were the USA and the EU. The former is the world's major food exporter and had to compete in world markets with heavily subsidized European food exports (see the next chapter). So the USA wanted to see the EU's agricultural policy remodelled to remove these dumped surpluses and offered to reform its own system of protecting agriculture. In the event, GATT negotiations ground on and on, not producing a new agreement until December 1993, almost three years beyond the original deadline. As will be examined in the next chapter, major agricultural concessions testify to the importance of trade to the EU.

Conclusion

Freer trade has been achieved both within the Single Market and with the rest of the world. In the Single Market the key has been mutual recognition. Mutual recognition applies to individuals, food, goods and services. For example, an accountant or any other professional who is qualified in one member state can work in any of the others. Fiscal and social harmonization remain as competition distorting problems.

KEY WORDS

Harmonization	European Central Bank
Non-tariff barriers	Tax harmonization
Competition	European Social Fund
Dominant position	Social Charter
Single European Act	Social Chapter
1992 Programme	External trade
Public procurement	GATT
Single European Document	Most-favoured nation
Mutual recognition	Uruguay Round
Subsidiarity	

Reading list

Anderton, A., Unit 88 in *Economics*, Causeway Press, 1991.
Bennett, P. and Cave, M., Chapter 3 in *Competition Policy*, Heinemann Educational, 1991.

Cook, M. and Healy, N., Chapter 4 in *Current Topics in International Economics*, Anforme, 1990.

Huhne, C., *Real World Economics*, Penguin, 1990, pp. 307–13.

Essay topics

1. What are the advantages and limitations of establishing a free trade area? How far do these apply to the European Economic Area established in 1991? (Joint paper, Oxford & Cambridge SEB/ Cambridge LES, AS Level, 1993)

2. Will the creation of a single European market in 1992 lead to fundamental changes in Britain's economic relationship with the European Community? (Oxford & Cambridge Schools Examination Board, 1990)

3. Define a market and explain why markets can improve economic welfare. Discuss how the Single European Market is intended to increase the economic welfare of the member states. (Northern Examinations and Assessment Board, 1992)

4. Examine the role of comparative advantage in determining what a country produces for international exchange. How is this concept relevant when analysing the effects of the creation of the Single European Market in 1992? (University of London Examinations and Assessment Council, 1992)

5. Discuss whether customs unions, such as the European Community, help or hinder the development of world trade in accordance with the principle of comparative advantage. (Associated Examining Board, 1992)

6. Explain the theoretical advantages and disadvantages of a customs union. How might the completion of the Single European Market affect the UK economy? (University of Cambridge Local Examinations Syndicate, AS Level, 1991)

Data Response Question 3

Competition and innovation in the European Community

This task is based on a question set by the Associated Examining Board in 1991. Read the article below which is adapted from *Competition and Innovation* by G.A. Geroski (an internal economic paper for the Commission of the European Communities), and answer the questions that follow.

1. Explain, in your own words, what the writer means by the terms: (i) dynamic efficiency, (ii) static efficiency, and (iii) monopoly power.

2. Explain why it seems reasonable to argue that: (i) 'increases in market size will increase innovation', and (ii) 'large firms with at least some degree of monopoly power are likely to be most innovative'.
3. Discuss the view that removing all barriers to trade within the European Community will bring substantial gains to all member states.

There are a number of obstacles which restrict trade within the European Community, and there are good reasons to think that removing them may bring substantial gains to all member states. Policies have been suggested to tackle these problems, and if adopted they are likely to improve the allocation of resources within the European Community.

The primary effects of reducing the barriers to trade between countries who are members of the European Community will be an increase in market size and in the amount of competition in the enlarged market. These changes are likely to affect the efficiency of firms and the performance of markets in several different ways. When examining these effects, it is necessary to distinguish between **dynamic efficiency** and **static efficiency**.

Improvements in dynamic efficiency will result if the removal of barriers to trade leads to invention, innovation and a faster rate of technological change. However even if these long run benefits do not occur it is still almost certain that there will be improvements in static efficiency. A larger market and more competition is likely to result in a better allocation of resources, even if the pace of technological change is unaffected. The only controversy is about the size of the benefits which will result from these improvements in static efficiency.

A larger market and the resulting increase in demand will allow firms with unexploited economies of scale to move down their long run average cost curves. More competition is also likely to encourage firms to reduce inefficiency and to produce whatever output they choose, at the lowest average cost. These two effects lead to the prediction that costs are likely to fall as the size of the market and the degree of competition increase.

The effects of market size and competition on dynamic efficiency, however, are much less clear. Certainly it seems reasonable to suggest that **increases in market size will increase innovation,** particularly if there are any economies of scale or fixed costs in the research and development process. However the effect of competition on innovation is rather controversial, some economists believe that **large firms with at least some degree of monopoly power are likely to be most innovative**. If this is true, it is not certain that removing the barriers to trade between the members of the European Community will improve dynamic efficiency. Indeed it is possible that the static efficiency gains will be more than outweighed by the losses arising from a reduction in dynamic efficiency.

Chapter Four

The Common Agricultural Policy (CAP)

A market-rigging monument to economic folly

This chapter examines the policy developed in the original EEC of Six countries and its modifications to the end of 1993.

When the EEC began in 1958 about 20 per cent of its population was employed in agriculture, making this by far the largest industry. Each member state had its own agricultural policy. Harmonizing these policies was essential, otherwise they would result in different food prices in different countries, and this would distort competition – because wages are influenced by food prices.

The need to develop a common agricultural policy is stated in Article 3 of the Treaty of Rome. It is the first common policy mentioned, underlining the importance attached to it.

The need to unify existing disparate national policies is obvious, but why were agricultural policies needed anyway?

Reasons for agricultural policies

In medieval times, most of the population were occupied by agriculture. The process of economic development involves the transfer of much of this labour force to other activities. Necessarily, the first requirement is for an increase in *labour productivity* in agriculture, so that some labour can be released.

In practice, *land productivity* increased along with that of labour, as food production increased, and food prices declined. Consequently the returns to agricultural resources in general declined. So resources were reallocated from agriculture to more profitable uses.

History demonstrates that labour is persuaded to leave agriculture only slowly, resulting in incomes that are persistently below those of other occupations. In the twentieth century, low incomes for such a large sector of the economy came to be considered as *inequitable,* and so became the focus for government intervention. The low incomes are caused by economic forces, but policies to raise them are *social,* not economic, although there are significant economic consequences.

An economic reason for intervention is that agricultural prices are inherently *unstable* in a free market. **Price elasticities** of demand for food products are low – because consumption of food means physical consumption, and once people are full a reduction in prices will not persuade them to eat much more. Neither will a rise in price greatly reduce their desire to eat.

Imagine that the price elasticity of demand for potatoes is –0.1, and in a particular year the yield of potatoes is low owing to drought and marketed output is reduced by 5 per cent. Clearly potato prices will rise and farmers can do nothing about it; extra potatoes can only be produced *next* year (i.e. the supply is perfectly inelastic in the short run). By how much will prices rise? – with these data, 50 per cent.

Thus, if the price elasticity of demand is low, which it is for most agricultural products, small changes in outputs cause relatively large changes in prices. Such unstable prices fail to tell producers what consumers really want. Some action to stabilize prices is therefore likely to result in an improvement in **economic efficiency.**

There is also a *strategic argument* for intervention. A secure food supply is an essential element of policy for any government and is neglected at a country's peril. The UK discovered this in the early years of this century. Comparative advantage had been followed, resulting in the UK exporting manufactures and importing food – a sound economic policy which seemed safe as there had been peace in Europe for a hundred years. When the First World War began in 1914, three-quarters of the flour in British bread was imported!

The Common Agricultural Policy

The aims of the policy as stated in Article 39 may be summarized as follows:

- to increase productivity
- to raise farm incomes
- to stabilize markets
- to assure the availability of supplies
- to ensure reasonable prices for consumers.

Although the Treaty of Rome does not make it clear, the fundamental objective is the raising of farm incomes, and we now turn to the methods of achieving this – *raising product prices* and *encouraging structural change.*

Price support

The EEC decided that farmers' incomes were too low because their product prices were too low, and so it designed a policy to raise prices.

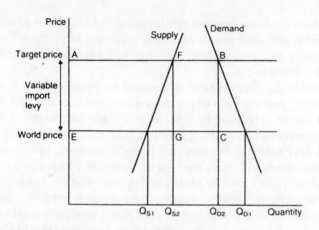

Figure 2 The *intended* operation of CAP price supports

Figure 2 relates to the situation in the 1960s when the policy was introduced. The supply and demand curves relate to EEC farmers and consumers. Free trade would result in a European price level of WP, standing for World Price. At this price Q_{S1} and Q_{D1} would be produced and consumed respectively, the difference being imported. The EEC decided to raise the wholesale price to TP (**target price**). At this price farmers expand production to Q_{S2} and consumption declines to Q_{D2}. Cheap imports are prevented from undermining the target price by a **variable import levy** (VIL) which raises WP to at least TP. The effects of the policy are to raise prices substantially – TP is much higher than WP – for the benefit of farmers. Prices are also stabilized, for if WP varies, the variable import levy is altered to compensate, thus keeping TP virtually constant. Consumers are worse off since they have to pay higher prices for less consumption; indeed, the area ABCE (price difference times consumption) is an **implicit food tax.** Area FBCG (variable import levy times quantity imported) represents the revenue collected on imports which reduces the need for other taxation. The policy evidently transfers income from food consumers to farmers and taxpayers. Of course, countries supplying imports are worse off as their market is diminished.

This support policy ignored time and the changes which it brings. Although the internal demand for food changed very little, since the population remained almost constant, supplies continually expanded under the spur of technological progress, encouraged by the artificially high level of prices.

So in Figure 3 the supply curve has moved to the right; and, at the

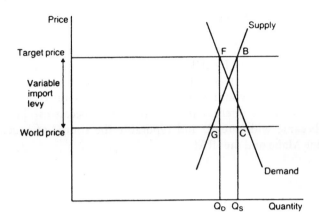

Figure 3 CAP price support in practice (cf. Figure 2)

administered price TP, production exceeds consumption even in the absence of imports. Originally the policy raised prices by reducing imports; when imports have been reduced to zero as in this figure, what is to stop price falling below TP to the level indicated by the intersection of demand and supply? – an **intervention system**.

It was realized from the beginning that for many products a post-harvest glut would force market prices below TP even without imports. An intervention agency in each member state was formed to buy and store produce at intervention prices – set a little below target prices. Later in the season there would be seasonal shortages, permitting the sale of the post-harvest surpluses.

But the situation in Figure 3 became the rule: supplies increased so much that surpluses were 'normal' instead of seasonal, and they were purchased and stored with little likelihood of future release on to the internal market. These surpluses became known popularly as butter, beef and cereals *mountains* and wine *lakes*. Other products were also in surplus: there have been vegetable oil lakes and dried currant mountains for example.

Comparing Figures 2 and 3, the major change is from net imports to surpluses. What became of the latter?

Most surpluses were exported. To make this possible, **export subsidies** were provided equal to TP minus WP, enabling traders to sell in world markets at world prices. Clearly this still involved a transfer of income from consumers to farmers, but now taxpayers had to pay for the removal of surpluses. Such 'dumping' (i.e. selling abroad below cost) of EC surpluses disadvantaged third countries supplying food to the world market. On the other hand many food importers got marvellous bargains.

It should be noted that this price policy did nothing to make farming competitive in world terms. Indeed, it accepted that European farming is uncompetitive and protected farmers from competition, which ensured that they never would become competitive. The difference in price levels between the internal and world markets became so large that fraud became widespread, and reputably the source of much income for the Mafia and the IRA!

Structural policy

Why was and is European agriculture uncompetitive? History bequeathed to Europe a very large number of farms, most being far too small to provide a reasonable income: small farms have high unit costs and produce little revenue. A farm can only expand to become a profitable business by increasing its land area, and as the supply of land is fixed it follows that an efficient agricultural industry means far fewer farms and *farmers*.

Here, then, is the problem: there were, and are, millions of farmers, most of whom would need to leave the land before agriculture could become efficient. But agricultural labour mobility is notoriously low, and as farmers die, or retire, too many are replaced by a new generation.

Since the 1960s, to increase mobility, there have been measures for retraining farmers for other occupations or to help them to retire. But few wish to leave agriculture and too little money has been provided for this **structural policy** to have much impact. Enthusiasm for such policies was notably lacking in the early days of the EEC when the economies of the Six were expanding rapidly. The widespread unemployment of more recent years has made any restructuring of farming far more difficult. Quite simply, there have been no jobs for ex-farmers to go to; *they might as well farm inefficiently as become unemployed.*

Green currencies

The price support policy was completed in 1968 – that is, agricultural prices in the member states had been gradually changed until they reached common levels. But then, events conspired to upset these common prices.

A world system of fixed exchange rates had operated successfully for about 24 years, now it began to break up. The common prices for agricultural products were denominated in units of account (now **European Currency Units**) which translated into member states' currencies at fixed rates. In 1969 the French franc was devalued and the

German mark revalued. At the new currency values, *since agricultural prices were in units of account,* the prices of French agricultural products should have increased (there are now more francs per unit of account) whilst German prices should have fallen.

Neither country was willing to permit these price changes, the French saying that higher food prices were inflationary and the Germans that lower prices would reduce farmers' incomes unacceptably. So although all other industries had to put up with the consequences of the currency changes, the out-of-date currency values were retained in both countries just for agriculture; i.e. prices in France were lower and in Germany higher than the agreed common prices.

To prevent these price differences distorting trade in agricultural products, a system of border taxes and subsidies was introduced. These **monetary compensatory amounts** (MCAs) became increasingly important as currency changes became more frequent. As they permitted the use of artificial exchange rates for internal agricultural trade, these rates became known as **green currencies**.

It is ironic that in a common market, the size of the MCAs became so large that real price differences for agricultural products often exceeded those existing between member states before the EEC began. *This is clearly a serious distortion of competition – such price differences prevent the operation of comparative advantage.* MCAs were supposed to be abolished with the introduction of the Single Market at the end of 1992, but they haven't been. They remain to distort the Single Market, and their ultimate removal is being made more difficult as currency instability has become prevalent.

Consequences of the CAP

Have its policy objectives been achieved? Certainly productivity has increased, and supplies have been assured, both partly the result of high prices. The manipulated price system has also stabilized prices. What is 'reasonable' cannot be objectively defined, so it is a matter of opinion whether or not prices to consumers have been reasonable.

What is beyond doubt is that the primary objective of raising farm incomes to levels comparable to those of other sectors has not been achieved. Before the inception of the CAP, and today, farmers on average have incomes about half of those of the non-farming members of society; the policy has completely failed to improve their relative position.

Averages always hide much information. In the present case consider who benefits most from higher prices – clearly the farmers who produce most. These large farmers also have lower unit production costs (economies of size). *So the CAP has been helping the larger, relatively wealthy farmers, whilst leaving the poorer small farmers still poor.* Also, the policy has transferred income from consumers to producers, including transfers from poor consumers – for even the poor must eat – to richer farmers! On equity grounds such income transfers have few supporters.

There are two other major areas affected by the CAP which must be considered: the financial and economic consequences.

Financial consequences

These arise from the need to dispose of the surpluses generated by the high-price system. These financial costs are met by the **Agricultural Guarantee and Guidance Fund** (universally known by the acronym FEOGA from its title in French) which has consistently dominated the budget, as shown in Table 5. So large is the expenditure on agricultural support that little has been left to finance other common policies. Consequently, the development of other policy areas has been hindered.

Table 5 Budgetary expenditure of the EU, selected years 1971–92 (million Ecus)

	Agricultural fund	Social fund	Regional fund	Industry energy research	Administration	Other	Totals	Agriculture percentage share
1971	1884	57	-	65	132	152	2289	82
1975	4587	360	150	99	375	643	6214	74
1979	10736	596	672	288	864	1448	14603	74
1983	16331	801	2266	1216	1162	2990	24766	66
1987	23939	2542	2562	965	1740	3721	35469	67
1991	35458	4069	6309	2077	2828	6681	57422	62
1992	38462	4817	7579	2424	2927	6619	62828	61

Source: *European Economy*, vol. 54, 1993.

Economic efficiency

Here the economic consequences of the CAP are discussed in *conventional* terms, some *environmental* effects are discussed in Chapter 7.

The fact that agriculture is much more heavily protected/subsidized than other industries means that it uses some resources which could be used more profitably elsewhere. Thus on the grounds of efficiency there is significant **resource misallocation** within the EU. As the other industrialized countries outside the EU have their own agricultural support systems, some even more protective than the CAP, the misallocation is of global significance.

Fields that grow nothing yield lucrative harvest

For the past five years, Robert Sherriff and his wife Penny have been paid £27,000 a year for growing only grass on more than half their 600-acre farm. They will be paid as much as £42,000 this year.

Mr Sherriff is one of 35,000 arable farmers in Britain expected to apply for grants of up to £129 for every acre on which they do not plant crops. About 1.7 million acres, bigger than Lincolnshire, could be left fallow at a cost to the taxpayer of £200 million.

Faced with mounting food surpluses, Britain and other European Community states are paying farmers to grow nothing to counter years of paying them subsidies to grow too much.

The Sherriffs started harvesting cash rather than crops at Bayford, Hertfordshire, in 1988, when they volunteered with a few other pioneers for a five-year trial of the set-aside scheme. Since last year, set-aside has become virtually compulsory for arable farmers with more than 40 acres.

'I was attracted by the security of income,' Mr Sherriff said. 'There was a lot of talk in 1988 of agricultural reform and even of doing away with price support.

Setaside offered a guaranteed £88 an acre for doing nothing except mow the grass once a year. About 150 acres of the farm had always been marginal, low-yielding land anyway.'

Mr Sherriff put down to grass 300 acres that had previously grown wheat, beans and oilseed rape. With half the farm idle, he laid off the two farmhands he had employed and hires contractors for such work as ploughing and spraying. Economists believe that at least one farming job is lost for every 300 acres set aside.

This year, under the even more generous compulsory scheme, Mr Sherriff is thinking of setting aside up to 375 acres. He will be entitled to £129 an acre for 60 per cent of this fallow area and £88 an acre for the rest, a total of about £42,000.

By taking part of his land out of production, he will qualify for other grants on the crops he does grow: £77 for each of his 170 acres of wheat and £144 for each of his 55 acres of beans, a further £21,000. The money is guaranteed even if his crops fail.

Source: *The Times*, 21 March 1994

The protection of agriculture is believed to contribute to unemployment in EU manufacturing. It is argued that because the CAP expands EU agricultural production to the point of major dumping on world markets (the EU is the world's second largest exporter of agricultural products), it must make countries which have a comparative advantage in agricultural production poorer. As a result their imports of manufactures from the EU are reduced, and it follows that so is employment in manufacturing industry. This problem is compounded by high food prices in the EU which help to raise costs via wages in other industries and damage their international competitiveness.

CAP reform

The failure of the CAP to provide 'fair' incomes for the small farmers despite its vast cost has led to the universal recognition that reform is necessary. *Unfortunately the true economic costs are difficult to quantify and seem to make little impact on politicians; they therefore base their decisions almost entirely upon the financial costs although these are of secondary importance.* So reforms are aimed at reducing the budgetary costs without addressing the other ill effects of the policy.

The undesirable consequences of the CAP largely result from high prices, but reducing them significantly is regarded as politically unacceptable and politicians therefore sought other ways of reducing budgetary costs. In 1984 a **quota system** was introduced for milk. This limits the support for milk production to a predetermined quota output, with extra production attracting a much lower price. This reduces the surpluses which must be disposed of (as butter) and hence the costs. However, it still leaves the consumers paying high prices and supporting producers via an implicit food tax.

The **MacSharry Plan** (see the box) was conceived under the intense pressure of the Uruguay round of GATT trade negotiations. Initially the proposed reforms were too little for the USA and too much for the French. After protracted and often heated US–EU negotiations an eventual compromise gave a new GATT agreement on 15 December 1993, almost three years beyond the original deadline and eight years after the negotiations began.

The economic effects of the CAP reforms include lower food prices for consumers. This is a radical change because it transfers support costs from consumers to taxpayers. Lower agricultural prices and outputs will permit a more rational allocation of resources within the EU. The international allocation of resources will also be ameliorated by a reduction in the quantity of EU surpluses being dumped on the world market.

The redistributive effects of the reformed CAP will also be more equitable in that poor consumers will no longer have to pay such high food prices to support farmers. However, the benefits to farmers will still accrue largely to the richer farmers. In 1991 MacSharry proposed a ceiling on individual farmer receipts of the direct income payments which his plan was to introduce. The UK government complained that such an arrangement would discriminate against its larger and more efficient farmers – it did not publicly comment that such farmers were also amongst the more wealthy or that they usually voted for the current government. *Thus the UK persuaded the EU to miss an opportunity to achieve a more equitable distribution of incomes within farming.*

The MacSharry reforms

'Major reforms', which turned out to be little more than tinkering, were agreed in 1988. The reforms introduced the quota principle to some of the major crops as a **stabilizer system**. This sought to stabilize outputs and financial costs by reducing the prices of outputs which exceeded set thresholds (notice how words like 'stabilize' and 'threshold' were used instead of politically less acceptable words like 'limit' and 'quota'). In the event, the thresholds set were too generous and the price reductions for above-threshold production were too timid for the stabilizer system to have much impact on output or support costs.

A voluntary **'set aside'** system was also introduced. This offered a subsidy to farmers who agreed to take some of their land out of production, thus reducing output. The rewards offered were too low to be attractive to farmers, so again the impact on output was negligible.

Agricultural Commissioner Ray MacSharry made much more radical reform proposals in 1991. After months of heated debate a modified version was adopted by the Council of Ministers in 1992.

The pivotal change was a phased reduction in cereal prices to bring them 'close' to world prices by 1997, with compensatory **direct income payments** being paid to farmers (approximately the price reduction times the average yield in the locality times the number of hectares grown). To receive compensatory payments a farmer had to agree to set aside at least 15 per cent of the farm's arable area. Set-aside land attracted a payment approximately equal to the profit foregone. Lower cereal prices imply reduced costs of animal feeds and the plan therefore included cuts in the prices of livestock products. (Except milk, for which the quota system is retained.)

The plan is remarkable because it attempts to replace politically manipulated prices with prices near to world market levels.

Conclusion

Until the early 1990s the EU avoided any significant reform of the CAP despite its obvious market-rigging folly, its vast expense and its failure to achieve its main income objective. However, the importance of trade to the EU turned out to be the lever which forced reform in the context of the Uruguay Round of GATT trade negotiations. Although output should in future be more subject to market forces, resource returns to land and farmers will still be heavily subsidized, and the distribution of the gains within farming will still be mainly to the richer farmers.

RIDDELL

KEY WORDS

Price elasticities	European Currency Units
Economic efficiency	Monetary Compensation
Price support	Amounts
Target price	Agricultural Guarantee and
Variable import levy	Guidance Fund
Implicit food tax	Resource misallocation
Intervention system	Quota system
Export subsidies	MacSharry Plan
Dumping	Stabilizer system
Structural policy	Set aside
Green currencies	Direct income payments

Reading list

Cook, M. and Healey, N., Chapter 3 in *Current Topics in International Economics*, Anforme, 1990.

Huhne, C., *Real World Economics*, Penguin, 1990, pp. 300–306.

Paisley, R. and Quillfeldt, J., Chapter 5 in *Economics Investigated*, vol. 2, Collins Educational, 1992.

Essay topics

1. Explain why the European Community needs a policy for agriculture. Discuss the economic reasons why reform of the Common Agricultural Policy (CAP) has been advocated. (University of Cambridge Local Examinations Syndicate, 1992)

2. Distinguish between comsumers' surplus, producers' surplus and economic rent. Discuss the effect on each of these if the government introduces a guaranteed minimum price for wheat above the free market equilibrium price. (University of Oxford Delegacy of Local Examinations, 1990)

3. Explain the case for government intervention in the determination of the prices received by farmers. Explain the consequences of two forms of such intervention. (University of London Examinations and Assessment Council, 1994)

4. Explain why the European Community needs a policy for agriculture. Discuss the economic reasons why reform of the Common Agricultural Policy (CAP) has been advocated. (University of Cambridge Local Examinations Syndicate, 1992)

5. Why do governments often protect and support the agricultural industry? Outline the main features of the European Community's Common Agricultural Policy. Discuss the principal costs and benefits of the Common Agricultural Policy. (Associated Examining Board, 1994)

Data Response Question 4
The CAP

This task is based on a question set by the Welsh Joint Education Committee in 1992. Read the article below, which is adapted from a piece in the *Financial Times* on 24 January 1991, and answer the questions that follow.

A slimmer sacred cow

Brussels has signalled that it is sizing up the most sacred of all European Community (EC) cows, the Common Agricultural Policy (CAP) farm subsidies regime, not to slaughter it, certainly, but to slim it down substantially.

Mr Ray MacSharry, the EC's Agriculture Commissioner, is calling for severe cuts in Community subsidies to farmers and smaller production quotas to stop them producing far more than the EC consumes.

He foresaw EC farm spending rising this year by about 7 billion European Currency Units (Ecus), or by 25 per cent, to over 32 billion Ecus, nearly 60 per cent of the Community budget. In 1992 it would rise further by 12.5 per cent. By the end of this month, EC-held beef stocks will have increased to 930 000 tonnes, comfortably over 1987's high of 800 000 tonnes: butter, skimmed milk and cereals are on the same mountain path.

It is the growing cost of a system which concentrates upon price support and rewards ever-greater output whatever the market demands, which is at the root of the reform drive.

The intervention price for cereals would drop from Ecu 169 to Ecu 90 a tonne, a 47 per cent cut. The subsidised price for beef would fall by 15 per cent and for milk by 10 per cent, with the milk quota for the EC as a whole being cut by 5 per cent.

The CAP, beyond its post-war aim of food self-sufficiency – long since achieved – always was part of social policy to help smaller farmers stay in business. It merely operated in an anti-social way: 60 per cent of cereals output is produced by 6 per cent of cereal farmers, who take 60 per cent of the subsidy even though they are highly competitive. In milk and beef the same sort of ratios occur.

---

1. Explain the basic purposes of the Common Agricultural Policy.
2. Why has the CAP led to the EU holding ever-larger stocks of beef, butter and other agricultural products?
3. Why might CAP subsidies be regarded as an inefficient use of EU revenues?
4. What are the likely effects of reducing the intervention prices and production quotas?

Chapter Five

Regional policy

The exploitation of comparative advantage may result in a regionally inequitable distribution of gains.

Chapters 2 and 3 dealt with the economic gains which were to flow from the introduction of free trade within Europe, both theoretically and in practice, particularly via the Single Market and wider European Economic Area. Free trade permits efficiency and the maximization of total income within the Union, but what about the distribution of that income? The effects on various groups – local, regional or national – may exacerbate existing inequalities. This chapter considers why the gains from the exploitation of comparative advantage may be distributed inequitably, and the consequent need for redistributive intervention. Regional policy should be seen as the first explicitly redistributive aspect of the EU. We now turn to the nature and causes of regional problems and the common policies designed to ameliorate them.

The nature and causes of regional problems
The major features of regional problems are relatively low incomes, low productivity and high unemployment. Clearly these are inter-related. They are caused by a variety of **market imperfections.**

- Firstly, in the real world perfect mobility of factors or products does not exist. So locational factors become very important. These include access to large markets, access to inputs (raw materials, centres of administrative or financial expertise), access to skilled labour.
- Secondly, comparing labour markets in different regions, wage differentials sometimes exceed productivity differences. Thus 'efficiency wages' (wages divided by productivity) can vary considerably, effectively rendering some regions uncompetitive.
- Thirdly, labour is not perfectly mobile. In practice the least skilled labour is least mobile. Conversely, the most skilled labour generally is mobile and leaves poor regions for employment in richer regions. These differences in labour mobilities exacerbate any initial regional income disparity.

A region may become depressed through some autonomous change in demand or supply or by the interplay of market forces. In the EU context, comparative advantage benefits the more efficient firms which expand their outputs and supplant the less efficient firms. Expansion and contraction are opposite sides of the same coin. Because of the market imperfections noted above, the gainers and losers from the Single Market tend to be regionally concentrated. A depressed region is unattractive to entrepreneurs and therefore lacks investment, so the depression becomes cumulative.

There is no reason to expect market forces to correct regional imbalances. Regional income disparities are thus a form of **market failure** and government intervention is essential to their amelioration.

When one country becomes depressed relative to others with which it trades it is able to restore its competitiveness by depreciating its currency. Regions within a country are unable to help themselves to adjust in this fashion because they belong to a single-currency nation. In future, when the Union becomes a single-currency group of nations each will have lost the exchange rate method of overcoming a loss of competitiveness. Evidently, a future EMU will make regional policy extremely important.

In the early 1990s, national income disparities are substantial. International comparisons of living standards are fraught with difficulty, but comparisons of GDP per head in terms of '**purchasing power standards**' give a reasonably fair indication. On this basis the eight richest members of the Union are reasonably close together, enjoying incomes significantly higher than those of the poorer four. In Greece and Portugal, GDP per head is about half that of the average of the eight. In Ireland and Spain, GDPs per head are about two-thirds and three-quarters respectively of the average of the eight. The poorest regions of the poorer countries have average incomes which are only a quarter of those of the richest regions of the richer countries.

There are two main types of depressed region:

- Rural areas where there is a heavy dependence upon agriculture, particularly if the farms are small leading to low labour productivity. Such areas are characterized by high unemployment and poorly developed infrastructures. The main low-income agricultural regions are the south of Italy, most of Greece, Ireland and Portugal and large areas of Spain.
- Urban areas where traditional industries, such as coal mining, steel production and ship-building are declining. The depressed urban regions typically suffer high unemployment, decaying housing and

infrastructures, and social deprivation. They are found largely in Belgium, France, the eastern part of the unified Germany, and the UK.

The evolution of regional policy

When the Union began in 1958 the original six members had their own regional policies. These national policies were generally intended to assist 'backward' regions, such as areas where traditional industries were in decline, to catch up with other areas. But at what level does assistance cease merely to compensate for regional disadvantages and become unfair national aids which distort competition?

Clearly some Union-level policy coordination was necessary if competitive forces were not to be negated. But in practice, so long as the Union enjoyed rapid economic growth and high overall employment, these issues were left to member states. Common policy was restricted to the establishment of the **European Investment Bank** (EIB). This was called for by Article 3 of the Treaty of Rome, largely with the south of Italy, the Mezzogiorno, in mind as the only major relatively poor area in the original Six .

Article 3 also called for the establishment of a European Social Fund (some aspects of social policy are discussed in Chapter 3). The ESF dealt with employment issues (particularly the retraining of workers displaced by structural change), leaving the main areas of social policy such as health, education, housing and pensions, to national authorities. EIB expenditures were, and still are, concentrated on improvements to infrastructures (improved roads, water supplies, etc.) in the poorer regions. The complementary nature of the expenditures of the ESF in these regions to improve working conditions and provide training – in short to raise labour productivity – make the Social Fund a part of regional policy.

In the early days of the CAP, its price-supporting activities were also thought of as having a regional role, in raising incomes in poor agricultural regions. As discussed in Chapter 4, the CAP tended in practice to favour the richer farmers in the richer regions and its price-distorting activities have been of little benefit in reducing regional income disparities. However, the Guidance Section of FEOGA does have a regional role and its assistance has been focused on the poorer agricultural regions. Guidance Section expenditure is now considered to be part of the regional structural funds.

The coincidence of EU enlargement problems, a reduction in the rate of economic growth and global depression in the mid 1970s increased general unemployment and left few opportunities for

Biggest EC hand-out goes to Britain

Britain continues to suffer the worst industrial decline in the European Community, the European Commission indicated yesterday.

The Commission announced areas that will qualify for aid in the next three years. Britain's total of £1.69 billion is the highest in the Community. To qualify for aid, areas.must have higher general and industrial unemployment rates than the EC averages.

Parts of London were designated areas of industrial decline for the first time for having some of the worst unemployment blackspots. Most of Scotland will gain, as will Tyne and Wear, Humberside, parts of the West Midlands and Gibraltar. Some aid goes to Durham, Greater Manchester, South Yorkshire, Cheshire and Cumbria.

Parts of the London boroughs of Enfield, Hackney, Haringey, Newham, Tower Hamlets and Waltham Forest will receive aid for the first time, as well as Thanet in Kent.

'It's very good news for London,' Bruce Millan, EC regional affairs commissioner said. 'For the first time it has been recognised by the Community that London has major problems'.

However, the Government said yesterday that it was 'disappointed' by the commission's aid allocation. Tim Sainsbury, the Industry Minister, said the allocation 'does not fully reflect' Britain's problems.

'We pressed the Commission to recognise the justification for a much greater coverage of urban areas,' he said. The Government is particularly concerned that large swaths of London and the East Thames corridor missed out, as well as Bristol, Derby and Leicester.

Although Britain's £1.69 billion is slightly less than in the last spending round four years ago, it is still more than any other EC country's allocation.

Source: *The Times*, 22 Dec. 1993

unemployed workers in poorer areas. Regional problems were thus highlighted, resulting in the establishment of the **European Regional Development Fund** (ERDF) in 1975. This was particularly welcomed by the UK which saw a regional policy as a means of obtaining some redistributive benefits to help in offsetting the large budgetary transfers resulting from CAP arrangements. Between 1975 and 1992 the UK received just over £4 billion from the ERDF which, although helping to offset CAP transfers, still left the UK as a major net contributor to the EU budget – a cumulative transfer of £17bn by 1992 (see Chapter 7). ERDF contributes towards matching national expenditures to stimulate the economic development or reconstruction of poorer regions.

The accession of Greece in 1981 and Portugal and Spain in 1986, all relatively poor countries, increased the importance of regional policies and EU expenditures increased substantially as shown in Table 6. At the same time the Single European Act envisaged the introduction of the Single Market which might increase existing regional disparities. Accordingly the SEA formally recognized the importance of regional redistribution and called for the coordination of existing policies and increased funding. The ERDF, ESF and the Guidance Section of FEOGA were grouped together as the **structural funds** whose activities were to be coordinated. The ERDF was to be the main instrument for reducing intra-EU disparities. In 1988 the European Council decided to double in real terms the resources devoted to structural funds over the next five years.

Table 6 Expenditures of the regional policy funds, selected years 1975-92

	European Investment Bank	European Regional Development Fund	European Social Fund
1975	814	150	360
1980	2384	752	502
1985	5699	1624	1413
1990	10996	4554	3212
1991	13672	6309	4069
1992	12974	7579	4817

Source: *European Economy, 55,* 1993.

By 1992, structural fund expenditures accounted for almost a quarter of the EU budget and represented 3.5, 2.9 and 2.3 per cent respectively of the GDPs of Portugal, Greece and Ireland. The extent of EU influence on regional investment is even greater than these figures suggest since matching funds have to come from national governments.

How does regional policy work?

At the beginning of this chapter the major problems were diagnosed as being poor location with respect to markets (i.e. high transport costs) and low labour productivity. It is at these two characteristics that expenditures have been targeted. The ESF focuses on retraining workers to raise their productivity, EIB loans and ERDF grants concentrate on improvements to infrastructures, particularly roads. Such expenditures have been largely in the poorer regions, especially of Greece, Portugal and Ireland, the three poorest members of the Union. *The thrust of the policy is to improve the economic environments of poor regions so that investment is attracted into them.*

The expanding importance of regional policy

Two further developments have occurred under the Treaty of Maastricht: the creation of a **Committee of Regions** and a **Cohesion Fund**. The latter will help countries where the GNP is less than 90 per cent of the EU average.

Use of the term 'cohesion' implies a link to economic and monetary union. When the latter removes monetary and exchange rate policies from national governments, whole member states, unable to adjust to changing economic circumstances, could become 'poorer regions'. Regional policy will then become one of several redistributive policies required to compensate for the inequitable distribution of incomes which the free market will generate.

In late 1993 the Commission acknowledged the growing importance of these problems by calling for a further expansion of resources devoted to the structural funds to raise them to *one third* of the EU budget.

The Delors White Paper

Jaques Delors, as President of the European Commission, presented his White Paper on *Growth, Competitiveness and Employment* to the European Council meeting in Brussels in December 1993. The document contains proposals for coordinated actions to increase economic growth and reduce unemployment. It is a plan aimed at the medium to long term.

The Commission is looking for an annual *growth* rate of at least 3 per cent up to the turn of the century. The main conditions to achieve this are a higher rate of investment – 23 to 24 per cent instead of the 19 per cent level of recent years – with a concomitant increase in savings and reduction in public sector deficits.

The financial cost of *unemployment* to member states in 1993 is estimated to be of the order of 210bn Ecu (£155 billion). Clearly a higher economic growth rate is fundamental to reducing unemployment, but other measures could also help. For example, member states could modify their employment legislation to reduce the non-wage costs of the lowly paid, thus encouraging job creation. Whilst some of the current high rate of unemployment is cyclical (i.e. due to the recession), too much is structural and technological. *Structural unemployment* is caused by rigidities in the system, such as the lack of geographical mobility as older industries decline, and regional policy is designed to address this problem. *Technological unemployment* is largely due to the speed of change: the new growth areas of information and communication, audiovisual technology and biotechnology require skills which are very different from those possessed by the labour force shed by declining industries, and adjustment in terms of developing appropriate skills is relatively slow. Much youth unemployment must be blamed on a shortage of education and training suited to the new industries. Clearly remedial policies must be largely national.

Both increased growth rates and reduced unemployment require improved **global competitiveness**. The main proposals to achieve this are 'public interventions' for the encouragement of growth markets, and the promotion of what the Commission calls 'immaterial' investment – research, training and know-how. For research, this implies expenditures on long-term fundamental research which are expected to result in the birth of the high-technology industries of the future. In the medium term, the **Trans-European Networks** are stressed as being important to both competitiveness and employment. These networks relate to transport, energy and telecommunications/information. Transport is the simplest example of what is envisaged: improved road, rail and air systems and links on a European rather than national geographic basis. This should reduce transport costs and thus help to overcome the locational disadvantages of poorer regions.

The Commission estimates that the White Paper programme needs financing at an annual rate of 20 bn Ecu for 1994–99. About 5.3 bn Ecu a year is already provided for in the budget (structural funds, cohesion funds and agreed provision for networks). A further 6.7 bn Ecu per year is being spent on these activities by the European Investment Bank. The Commission proposes making up the annual shortfall of about 8 bn Ecu by borrowing in the market ('Union Bonds') to expand the funds of the EIB.

Conclusion

Regional policy has its origins in the need to assist the poorer regions, both rural areas heavily dependent on small farms and urban areas with a concentration of declining industries. As European integration proceeds, the gains from the exploitation of comparative advantage tend to benefit some regions more than others; indeed the decline of some areas may be accelerated. Consequently redistributive regional policies are increasingly important. By 1992 such structural policies already accounted for a quarter of the EU budget, with further substantial increases called for in the Delors White Paper. The further integration represented by economic and monetary union, examined in the next chapter, will greatly expand the role of regional and other redistributive policies.

```
┌─────────────────────────────────────────────────────┐
│                    KEY WORDS                          │
│                                                       │
│  Market imperfections        Structural funds         │
│  Market failure              Committee of Regions     │
│  Purchasing power            Cohesion Fund            │
│  European Investment Bank    Global competitiveness   │
│  European Regional           Trans-European Networks  │
│    Development Fund                                    │
└─────────────────────────────────────────────────────┘
```

Reading list

Goodman, S., 'The Community's regional policy', section 8 in *British Economy Survey*, Longman, autumn 1993.

Smith, D., Chapter 9 in *UK Current Economic Policy*, Heinemann Educational, 1994.

Essay topics

1. To what extent may developments within the European Community exacerbate regional problems within the United Kingdom? (University of Oxford Delegacy of Local Examinations, 1992)
2. 'Current regional policy offers no solution to the growing problem of long-term unemployment.' Discuss this statement. (Oxford & Cambridge Schools Examination Board, 1992)

Data Response Question 5

The North-South divide

This task is based on a question set by the University of London Examinations and Assessment Council in 1991. Table A shows some economic indicators from different regions in Great Britain, while Table B shows the relative importance of the manufacturing sector in the regions. Study the two tables and answer the questions that follow.

1. Examine the proposition that living standards in the 1980s were higher in the South than in the North.
2. What problems arise in using data for a whole region such as shown here?
3. How do the data in Table B help to explain the existence of regional disparity?
4. Suggest *two* 'active' policies available to the government to reduce regional disparities.

5. Examine one other indicator *not* given in Table A or Table B which could also be used to illustrate regional differences.

Table A Economic indicators

	GDP pc[a]	GDP pc[a] (1975 = 100)	Average weekly earnings[b]	Unemployment[c]	Long-term unemployment[d]
The 'South':					
South East	£5831	114.7	£248	8.5%	36.2%
South West	£4763	93.9	£209	10.4%	32.7%
East Anglia	£5118	100.7	£205	9.3%	33.5%
The 'North':					
East Midlands	£4861	95.7	£203	11.4%	39.2%
West Midlands	£4690	92.3	£192	13.8%	46.3%
Yorks. & Humbs.	£4662	91.8	£179	13.8%	42.0%
North	£4717	92.9	£170	16.9%	44.3%
North West	£4877	96.0	£183	14.3%	44.3%
Wales	£4509	88.9	£187	14.3%	40.6%
Scotland	£4942	97.4	£198	15.1%	39.2%

Notes: a Gross Domestic Product per capita, 1985.
　　　　b Average pre-tax weekly earnings per household, 1984–85.
　　　　c As a percentage of working population, January 1987.
　　　　d As a percentage of registered unemployed, January 1987.

Source: N. Healey, 'The North-South divide: rhetoric and reality', *Economics,* summer 1988.

Table B The manufacturing sector

	Manufacturing as % total employment in 1979	Percentage change 1979–86 in total employment in:	
		Manufacturing	Non-manufacturing
The 'South':			
South East	25.0	−25.4	+6.2
South West	27.5	−14.8	+3.2
East Anglia	29.3	−2.4	+13.1
The 'North':			
East Midlands	39.0	−18.0	+7.5
West Midlands	44.0	−28.6	+4.9
Yorks. & Humbs.	35.2	−35.0	+1.1
North	32.9	−34.1	−3.7
North West	36.3	−34.7	−4.5
Wales	30.5	−35.9	−8.6
Scotland	28.7	−31.8	−1.5

Source: H. Armstrong and J. Taylor, *Regional Policy: the Way Forward*, Employment Institute, 1987.

Chapter Six
Economic and monetary union

One market ... one money

Economic and monetary union is the final stage in economic integration; it alone will enable the EU to capture *all* of the benefits of the Single Market. It means the replacement of national currencies with a single European currency and centralized control of monetary and economic policies. *It involves such a pooling of sovereignty that political union is the only logical conclusion.*

The EMU debate
There is a limit to the degree of market integration which can be achieved so long as national currencies and economic policies exist. Even in the absence of tariff barriers, and if all technical standards and company law were harmonized and all non-tariff barriers removed, national currencies would still inhibit competition in two ways:

- The conversion of one currency into another adds to costs.
- The possibility that the exchange rates between currencies may change during a deal adds substantially to uncertainty. This is magnified by differences in inflation rates.

Finally, different economic policies in member states result in different rates of interest and different methods and rates of taxation for both companies and consumers. It follows that the full benefits of the internal market can only be achieved by full economic and monetary union.

Brief mention should be made here of the CAP. One of its problems has been that of uncommon prices caused by the 'green' currency exchange rate system. A common currency would resolve this difficulty and ease the operation of the CAP in either its old or reformed state.

What is the economic case against EMU?
Take the case of a member country with balance of payments problems causing its exchange rate to fall. It has three policy options:

- Use its reserves of gold and foreign currency to support its desired exchange rate.

- Raise its interest rate to increase the international demand for its currency.
- Cure the underlying problem. For example, it may be that a high inflation rate is making the country uncompetitive and anti-inflationary policies are required.

Any or all of these policies may fail and then equilibrium must be restored by altering the exchange rate, or permitting it to be determined by market forces. If the country in question is locked into an EMU, it possesses none of these options – its currency is the common currency, fixed in terms of its partners, and it has the same rate of inflation as its partners. So if its workers demand higher wages and fail to increase productivity accordingly, they will become unemployed; national economic policy has no power beyond that of persuasion to help them.

In reality these arguments against EMU are political in that control over economic policy instruments is lost by individual countries. This loss of control is indeed very substantial. The possibility of one country becoming depressed relative to the others implies corrective action involving considerable resource transfers; ultimately redistributive regional policies as part of a central budget and central economic policy control would be essential.

As the EMU debate turns out to be largely political, the present discussion must avoid taking sides and will concentrate on the economic issues. These deal with how EMU may be achieved, and charts developments.

How can EMU be achieved?

There are four essential elements to EMU:

- a single currency
- an EU central bank
- an EU economic policy
- EU political control.

A single currency, the first hurdle, is the one which appears to attract most attention – not surprisingly, for once this has been agreed the other elements of EMU must follow.

The transition towards EMU would be very disruptive if economic conditions between member states differed much when a single currency was introduced. Consequently detailed **convergence criteria** have been agreed. They are set out in the Maastricht Treaty, and continue the general direction of **cohesion policy** followed since EMU was called for in the Single European Act. Each member state should satisfy the criteria before joining the EMU. The criteria relate to:

- price stability
- favourable interest rates
- stable exchange rates
- reasonable level of government debt.

Price stability is defined as an annual rate of inflation which is no more than 1.5 per cent above that of the average of the three best performing member states. A favourable interest rate is similarly defined except that the permitted maximum difference is 2 per cent. A stable exchange rate means a narrow-band ERM rate (see below) which has been sustained for at least two years. Finally, government debt must be no more than 60 per cent of GDP. We now turn to the common cooperative attempt to stabilize exchange rates.

The European Monetary System (EMS)

The EMS was introduced in 1979 with two main aims: first to increase economic convergence, and second to create a zone of monetary stability within the Community to foster internal trade. Of course these aims have to be seen against the long-term aim of EMU to which they would contribute.

As part of the EMS each member state (including the UK) handed 20 per cent of its gold and foreign currency reserves to the **European Monetary Cooperation Fund** in return for Ecus (discussed below). These can be used in transactions within the EU. The Ecu (**European Currency Unit**) was introduced (replacing the very similar European Unit of Account) as a composite currency; i.e. it is a unit based on a 'weighted basket' of members' currencies. The weight assigned to each currency is in proportion to the relative size of that country's economy. As Germany is the largest economy in the Community it has a large weight in the Ecu. The composition of the Ecu was reviewed every few years, but it was fixed when the Maastricht Treaty came into force (see Table 7).

The **Exchange Rate Mechanism** (ERM) is the central part of the EMS and its operation is intended to provide a zone of monetary stability. The currency of each member has a specific value (**parity**) in terms of the Ecu. In turn this means that each currency has a parity value in terms of each of the other member currencies. Any one currency is permitted to vary by plus or minus 2.25 per cent against any other member currency. When this margin is reached the two central banks concerned must intervene to keep within the limits.

Table 7 Composition of the Ecu from 21 September 1989

Currency	Amount in national currency	Percentage weights
Belgian/Luxembourg franc	3.431	8.28
Danish krone	0.1976	2.58
German mark	0.6242	32.63
Greek drachma	1.440	0.53
Spanish peseta	6.885	4.50
French franc	1.332	19.89
Irish punt	0.008552	1.08
Italian lira	151.8	8.18
Dutch guilder	0.2198	10.23
Portugese escuda	1.393	0.71
British pound	0.08784	11.45
Totals	1.0 Ecu	100.00

Notes: The monetary amounts are those defined on 21.9.89 and are frozen up to stage 3. The weights will change every time the exchange rate of one currency changes – appreciating currencies' weights will increase and vice versa – so the actual value of the Ecu can change over time.
Source: Press Release, Brussels, 8 November 1993

There is a second element to the mechanism, a **divergence indicator.** This is three-quarters of a country's permitted variation against the Ecu. When this indicator is reached the country is expected to take corrective action. Thus if the currency falls in value the government might increase interest rates, increase taxation or support the currency.

By 1989 only the three poorest southern European member states – Greece, Portugal and Spain – together with the UK, had not joined the ERM. The three intended to join as soon as their economic circumstances permitted; Spain did so in 1989 and Portugal in 1992, both with 6 per cent permitted bands of variation against their central parity.

In the UK, political opposition to the ERM, because it was seen as yet another sacrifice of sovereignty, militated against joining. However, against the will of many on the right of the government, the UK joined in October 1990. The sterling exchange rate at which the UK chose to join was regarded by many as too high, a subject which is discussed in Chapter 7.

Appraisal of the EMS

The objectives of the EMS are economic convergence and stability, important prerequisites for economic and monetary union.

Real convergence is the convergence of EU economies to the highest current EU living standards through the catching up of the poorer countries and regions. The EMS cannot directly cause this convergence but it can help to produce the stable economic environment in which real convergence can occur, helped by the cohesion policy.

Nominal convergence implies convergence towards the lowest rates of inflation, and to balance of payments and budget balances which together encourage more stable exchange rates – the ideal prelude to EMU is exchange rates which are so stable that they can be fixed, and replaced with a single currency.

Rates of inflation are one of the main indicators of nominal convergence. Table 8 indicates that countries with high inflation rates have reduced them towards the EU average. Recession at the end of the 1980s, together with the monetary consequences of German reunification in 1990, have slowed progress. Data for USA and Japan are given for comparison.

Table 8 Rates of inflation in the EU, 1985 and 1993

	1985	1993		1985	1993
Belgium	5.9	2.8	Luxembourg	4.3	3.6
Denmark	4.3	1.4	Netherlands	2.2	2.1
West Germany	2.1	3.3	Portugal	19.4	6.7
Greece	18.3	13.7	**UK**	5.3	3.4
Spain	8.2	4.7	**EUR12**	5.9	3.7
France	6.0	2.3			
Ireland	5.0	2.3	USA	3.3	2.9
Italy	9.0	4.4	Japan	2.2	1.3

Source: *European Economy, 55,* 1993.

So long as inflation rates differ between member states there will be strains in the EMS. Accordingly there have been various alterations in exchange rates, countries with the higher inflation rates devaluing and those with lower rates revaluing. This has provided an incentive for countries to keep inflation low to retain their competitive positions compared with fellow members.

Another significant strain in the EMS is the difference in relative attractivenesses of members' currencies. Whenever there is pressure on

Speculators humiliate ERM

Currency speculators and international investors celebrated victory over the European Community yesterday, as weak currencies in the now defunct European exchange rate mechanism were savaged and Germany was angrily blamed for the system's collapse.

European politicians said Germany had failed to respect its obligations in the ERM and had triggered its death. The European Commission warned that the dismantling of the ERM and its economic consequences threatened to put countries at each others' throats and wreck the single market.

The ERM was pronounced all but dead after the meeting of finance ministers and central bank governors broke up early on Monday morning. They let all currencies apart from the German mark and Dutch guilder fluctuate by up to 15 per cent from their central rate. Economists said the widening of the bands was purely cosmetic and that Europe had re-adopted a system of floating exchange rates after 14 years in which the ERM had been the cornerstone of European economic co-operation.

Source: *The Independent*, 3 Aug. 1993

the American dollar, speculative funds flood into the deutchsmark, and this has been a factor in some exchange rate realignments. There were eleven realignments between 1979, when the ERM began, and 1987. Then no further changes took place until the Italian lira was devalued in 1990. The ERM was increasingly being regarded as significantly successful, despite the UK being forced out by speculative pressures in October 1992 (see Chapter 7).

But with little warning the whole system collapsed on 2 August 1993, again under intense speculative pressures. The boxed extract from *The Independent* details this, noting that widening the ERM bands to 15 per cent effectively introduced a system of floating exchange rates. The author of this article puts forward the view that the retention of the ERM is merely cosmetic, but in my opinion it is not – the important point to note is that the mechanism is still in place and at some future date there will be a return to narrow bands. This may well be in the context of changes in the *modus operandi* of the system, but the reconstruction of the ERM will go ahead – *for a system of stable exchange rates is still essential to the goal of EMU.*

The EMU timetable

The European Council has adopted a **three-stage timetable**. Stage 1 began in July 1990. During this stage the aim was to encourage further economic convergence, price stability, and sound public finance. The cohesion policy designed to raise the economic circumstances of the poorer Union members towards those of the richer members – discussed in the previous chapter – is a major element.

Progress in this stage has been slowed by the higher than expected costs of German reunification, which raised inflation and interest rates throughout the EU, and by widespread recession.

Stage 2 was agreed at Maastricht to start in 1994 with central banks and their activities as the focus of attention. Currently, most central banks are controlled directly or indirectly by their national governments; in this stage they are to become independent.

A **European Monetary Institute** (EMI) is being established as the precursor of a European Central Bank. The EMI is beginning its work in 1994 in Basle until suitable accommodation is ready in Frankfurt. The EMI aims to increase cooperation between members' central banks and to coordinate their monetary policies, to encourage the convergence of inflation and interest rates and help to stabilize exchange rates. In the latter context the EMI will be the major player in the reconstruction of the ERM. Finally the EMI will develop the use of the Ecu and introduce a clearing system for it.

These duties of the EMI could be summarized as guiding member states towards the attainment of the four convergence criteria which are fundamental to a smooth transition to EMU.

Stage 3 is economic and monetary union. By the end of 1996 the Commission and the EMI are to report on the progress of economic convergence. If a majority of members meet the four convergence criteria then the European Council, by qualified majority vote, can launch stage 3. If not enough members meet the criteria in 1996, stage 3 will be postponed until 1 January 1999. Then *members which do meet the criteria will proceed to full economic and monetary union,* leaving the other members outside the new union until they have caught up, their positions being reviewed every two years.

When EMU will actually occur is unknown, but the Treaty of Maastricht sets out its main elements. The EMI will be transmuted into the **European Central Bank** (ECB) which will be independent of the Commission, the European Parliament and national governments. The ECB will define and execute EU monetary policy, undertake its foreign exchange operations and hold its foreign reserves. Members' exchange rates will be fixed and their currencies replaced by the Ecu; the ECB will be the sole issuer of notes and coin.

Clearly EMU involves huge changes in sovereignty. Those against EMU describe it as an unacceptable loss of national sovereignty, those in favour consider it to be an essential pooling of sovereignty. All twelve EU members have signed and ratified the Maastricht Treaty and so presumably agree both with its timetable and ultimate destination. Well, ten members do. The UK has insisted on a protocol which leaves the final decision on its joining the EMU to be taken by a future government and parliament. Denmark, too, has been agreed an opt-out which is likely to leave its final decision to a national referendum.

Conclusion

These topics clearly raise both political and economic issues which must be kept apart in the mind of the economist. On the economic benefits of EMU an empirical study, *One Market, One Money,* published in November 1990 by the Commission (with the support and advice of several economists outside the Commission) produced some interesting conclusions. It expected EMU to reduce the rate of inflation, and since there will be one currency only, exchange rate transactions costs will be removed. Both of these factors will contribute to a significant reduction in uncertainty and so encourage an expansion in investment. The consequent increase in Union GDP will be of the order of 6 per cent and dynamic in nature – that is approximately equal to the economic benefits of the Single Market which were detailed in Chapter 2. These findings underline the strength of the economic case for EMU.

KEY WORDS

Convergence criteria	Divergence indicator
Cohesion policy	Real convergence
European Monetary	Nominal convergence
Cooperation Fund	Three-stage timetable
European Currency Unit	European Monetary Institute
Exchange Rate Mechanism	European Central Bank
Parity	

Reading list

Cook, M. and Healey, N., Chapters 2 and 7 in *Current Topics in International Economics*, Anforme, 1990.

Essay topics

1. Analyse the nature and means of monetary integration in the EC. Discuss why the UK has been a reluctant participant in this aspect of EC affairs. (University of Cambridge Local Examinations Syndicate, 1994)
2. Contrast the impact of monetary and fiscal policies which a government might use to rectify a worsening balance of payments on

current account. Has the UK's membership of the ERM affected the government's freedom of action in the use of these policies? (University of London Examinations and Assessment Council, 1992)

3. What exactly is meant by 'European Economic and Monetary Union'? Is such a goal either attainable or desirable? (Oxford & Cambridge Schools Examinations Board, 1992)

4. Why do some economists argue for fixed exchange rates whereas others are critical of such a system of exchange rate determination? (University of London Examinations and Assessment Council, 1994)

5. Outline the main features of the European Monetary System. Discuss the significance of membership of the EMS for the conduct of economic policy, illustrating your answer by referring to recent experience in the United Kingdom. (Associated Examining Board, 1993)

6. Define foreign exchange rates and explain what factors can cause them to fluctuate in the long term and the short term. Discuss the merits of the ERM and EMU, (a) to its members, and (b) to the rest of the world. (Northern Examinations and Assessment Board, 1993)

7. With the aid of the following data, examine the differences in living standards between the member states of the European Community. Discuss ways in which European Community policies seek to reduce these differences. (Joint paper, Oxford & Cambridge SEB/Cambridge LES, AS Level, 1992)

GNP per head in the European Community, 1989 ($US)

Belgium	16 220	Italy	15 120
Denmark	20 450	Luxembourg	18 500
France	17 820	Netherlands	15 920
Germany (West)	20 440	Portugal	4 250
Greece	5 350	Spain	9 330
Ireland	8 710	United Kingdom	14 610

Source: *World Development Report*, World Bank, 1991

Date Response Question 6
The Maastricht Treaty and EMU

This task is based on a question set by the Oxford and Cambridge Schools Examinations Board, 1993. Read the article, which is an adapted version of 'From EMS to EMU' by Andrew Britton (*IEA: The State of the Economy 1992*), and answer the questions that follow.

1. Give *three* examples of 'attempts to conduct an independent macroeconomic policy in Britain'.
2. Define (i) full employment; (ii) fiscal transfers; and (iii) regional and social funds.
3. What are the advantages of having a European central bank that is 'largely independent of government'?
4. What is meant by 'measures of convergence'? Why is such convergence seen as a precondition of EMU entry?
5. 'Clearly, any unified central mechanism must involve setting uniform interest rates'. Why?
6. Why will the rate of inflation 'not be identical in each country'?
7. Why does the author believe that Britain's path to full membership of EMU might be difficult? What options are open to a government to smooth this path?

Attempts to conduct an independent macroeconomic policy in Britain are now seen as a failure. A European monetary union, with a single currency, is now seen as the most reliable route to price stability.

The institutional framework for monetary union, as agreed at Maastricht, has been built mainly to a German model. The proposed European central bank will be **largely independent of government**, and therefore able to distance itself somewhat from political pressure. The overriding aim of monetary policy, written into the constitution of the bank, will be price stability – i.e. a rate of inflation of about 2 or 3 % a year. The Maastricht Treaty defines, precisely and arithmetically, just what **measures of convergence** are needed before individual countries are deemed fit to join a monetary union.

Clearly, any unified central mechanism must involve setting uniform interest rates. Indeed, the main instrument by which price stability will be secured will be the setting of these interest rates. Even in a monetary union, the rate of inflation will **not be identical in each country** and anxiety remains that the cost of achieving permanently low inflation will turn out to be very high for the countries with a history of relatively high inflation.

The case for monetary union rests on the belief that adjustments of imbalances between member countries is possible without changing exchange rates. Countries which become uncompetitive should reduce real wages or raise productivity so as to maintain or restore **full employment**. Within a nation state the problem of maintaining regional balance is solved in part by **fiscal transfers**, which help to narrow the regional dispersion of real incomes and employment levels. No such transfers are envisaged within the EMU. The Treaty makes provision for some enlargement of the **regional and social funds,** but these are not designed to bail out the industries of countries which fail to reduce inflation and thus price themselves out of the European market. These funds will therefore do nothing at all to ease Britain's path to full membership of EMU. Now that exchange rates cannot move to compensate for lack of competitiveness, the main burden of adjustment must rest with wage and price flexibility.

Chapter Seven

Impact of membership on the UK

This royal throne of kings, this scept'red isle
This earth of majesty, this seat of Mars,
This other Eden, demi-paradise,
. . . .
With inky blots, and rotten parchment bonds;
That England, that was wont to conquer others,
Hath made a shameful conquest of itself.

John of Gaunt in *Richard II*

There are still some in the UK who see membership of the European Union as the surrender of **sovereignty** – whether they are right or as out of date as John of Gaunt is a matter of personal opinion.

Political opinion in the UK remains split. Labour, Liberal Democrat, and a majority of Conservative Members of Parliament are pro-Europe, but a significant number of right-wing Conservatives are very strongly opposed, and frequently make difficulties for the government over all UK dealings with the EU.

The point is well illustrated by the following comments published in *The Spectator* on 14 July 1990; they were made by Mr Ridley, then Minister for the Environment:

> *'When I look at the institutions to which it is proposed that sovereignty is to be handed over, I'm aghast. Seventeen unelected reject politicians with no accountability to anybody, who are not responsible for raising taxes, just spending money, who are pandered to by a supine parliament which also is not responsible for raising taxes, already behaving with an arrogance I find breathtaking – the idea that one says, "OK, we'll give this lot our sovereignty", is unacceptable to me. I'm not against giving up sovereignty in principle, but not to this lot. You might just as well give it to Adolf Hitler, frankly.'*

After the publication of these views Mr Ridley was quickly forced to resign! Nevertheless many commentators claimed that Mr Ridley had only said in public what numerous politicians, including perhaps the then Prime Minister Mrs Thatcher, believed in private.

In November 1990 the deputy Prime Minister, Sir Geoffrey Howe, resigned his post on the grounds that he disagreed profoundly with Mrs Thatcher's approach to the EU. This encouraged Mr Heseltine, who had himself resigned from the Cabinet over a European issue some years previously, to challenge Mrs Thatcher for the Conservative party leadership. The subsequent election competition forced Mrs Thatcher to resign, and Mr John Major became the new Prime Minister.

These changes in the Conservative leadership failed to heal the divisions, which were soon exposed again in often vituperous debates over Maastricht. The accompanying boxed extract from *The European* sums up the right-wing case admirably.

Whatever his own views, Mr Major was unable to agree to all of the elements of the Maastricht Treaty because of his parliamentary right-wing. Specifically, he refused UK participation in the social policy (see Chapter 5), and insisted that any final decision on the UK joining a future EMU must be the prerogative of the government of the day. In the event, he was unable to persuade all of his right-wing MPs to vote with the government and ratification of the Maastricht Treaty was only possible because of the support of the Liberal Democrats – Labour voted against on the grounds that the UK should have accepted the whole of Maastricht rather than its mutilated remains (with the Social Chapter missed out, and an EMU opt-out put in).

These exciting political events underline the current importance attached to the relationship between the UK and the EU and the depth of controversy which this matter generates. They have been related here because it is essential for economists to recognize and take account of the political aspects of their analyses, but it must be emphasized that *in their economic analyses economists must remain as far as possible unbiased.* So we now turn from noting political events to asking the factual question – what then is the economic impact of EU membership?

It is evident that joining has greatly reduced the policy choices available to the British government. More and more decisions are taken by the Union jointly rather than by Britain independently. Thus if the UK has a balance of payments problem, membership rules out the use of import controls or subsidies to help UK firms. Competition policy is increasingly determined in Brussels. For some years all major policy decisions affecting agriculture have been taken at Union level. But common action can be very beneficial, and the single European market could only be achieved through collective decision-making.

As we have frequently noted, the UK government has not been happy at the prospect of more decisions being transferred to Brussels.

DEEP DIVISIONS OVER MAASTRICHT

Baroness Thatcher says why she sees the treaty as an outdated vision of Europe

Like many of my fellow Tories, I too have a favourite quotation from Disraeli. At Manchester in 1872 he said that "the programme of the Conservative Party is to maintain the Constitution of the country". This Conservative government, like its predecessors, should have as its main priority the maintenance of our constitutional freedoms, our democratic institutions, and the accountability of Parliament to the people. Because I believe in these principles so deeply I cannot support the ratification of the Maastricht treaty, and I welcome sterling's departure from the Exchange Rate Mechanism (ERM).

The treaty will hand over more powers to unelected bureaucrats, and erode the freedoms of ordinary men and women in this country. And no mere declaration on subsidiarity is going to change the Articles or the thrust of the treaty itself – even assuming that more notice is taken of such a declaration than of those I insisted be appended to the Single European Act.

Our political debate on the Maastricht treaty and the future development of Europe has been conducted in, if possible, even less rational terms than our discussion of exchange rates. We are warned from home and abroad, that it would be a national humiliation if Britain were left in the "slow lane" while others sped towards economic and monetary union. We risk being relegated, it is delicately hinted, to the "second tier" of a two-tier Europe. We must not miss the Continental Express. We must be at the "heart" of Europe. But, as Lord Salisbury once pointed out, half the errors in politics come from taking metaphors literally.

There have been two visions of Europe competing with each other in recent years. There is, first, the federalist vision of a Europe run increasingly from Brussels, united by a common citizenship, harmonised by bureaucratic regulations, equipped with common economic, budgetary, foreign and defence policies, using a single currency and acquiring all the flags, anthems and symbols of nation-hood: all in all, a United States of Europe in embryo.

Then there is what might be called the "con-federal" concept of a Europe of national states, based upon the idea of co-operation between independent sovereign countries loosely linked in a free trade area, with competition between different tax and regulatory systems and with freely floating currencies. This "con-federal" Europe would accommodate the countries of eastern Europe and give them a reasonable stability. It would maintain, not jeopardise, our relationship with Europe's great friend and protector, the United States.

It is time to get our priorities right. There are more urgent things for Europe to attend to now than Maastricht. It must further free trade by completing the Uruguay round of Gatt. It must strengthen links with America, inside and outside Nato. Above all, it must use both free trade and security to help ex-communist nations build prosperity and entrench freedom.

Britain needs to regain the confidence that we can manage our own affairs successfully once more. And we need a clearly defined economic policy to encourage soundly-based growth. Maastricht can do nothing to assist but much to damage progress towards those objectives. The government must recognise that Maastricht, like the ERM, is part of the vision of yesterday. It is time to set out the vision for tomorrow.

Baroness Thatcher was British Prime Minister from 1979 to 1990.

Source: *The European*, 8–11 Oct. 1992

The debate over economic and monetary union is the ultimate example of these concerns.

The economic benefits of membership

Table 9 gives some of the main economic indicators for the UK economy. It shows *three phases* of the UK rate of growth since accession to the Community in 1973.

In the first phase (1974–81), the rate of economic growth was much lower than in the decade before accession. Then in the 1980s economic growth resumed to average about 2.8 per cent, much better than in the 1970s but still less than the average of the 1960s. In the early 1990s the UK suffered negative growth (a contradiction in terms but conventional usage). What factors lay behind these changes in growth rates?

The 1974–81 low-growth period is not necessarily due to any negative impact of EC membership; it is easily explained by external events. In 1974 the world price of oil increased by almost 400 per cent, followed by further significant increases at the end of the decade. This was a major factor in precipitating a worldwide depression, so low growth rates were then the norm in all industrialized countries.

1979 saw the election of Mrs Thatcher's government and the introduction of radical economic ideas. That administration would

Table 9 Evolution of the UK economy, 1961–94

	1961 to 1973	1974 to 1985	1986	1987	1988	1989	1990	1991	1992	1993	1994*
GDP annual real growth rate(%)	3.2	1.4	4.3	4.8	5.0	2.2	0.4	–2.3	–0.5	1.9	2.5
Gross fixed capital formation (% share of GDP)	18.5	18.0	17.0	17.8	19.4	20.3	19.4	16.9	15.6	15.2	15.5
Inflation rate (%)	4.8	12.0	4.0	4.3	5.0	5.9	5.5	7.4	4.8	3.4	3.6
Productivity change (%)†	2.9	1.6	4.4	3.0	1.7	–0.4	–0.7	0.8	1.8	3.3	1.5
Real unit labour costs index	100.0	101.3	97.3	96.6	96.6	98.6	101.8	102.5	102.0	99.4	97.8
Employment annual change (%)	0.3	–0.2	–0.1	1.8	3.2	2.5	1.1	–3.1	–2.2	–1.3	0.9
Unemployment rate (%)	2.0	6.9	11.4	10.4	8.5	7.1	7.0	8.8	10.0	10.4	9.9

* Forecast. † GDP at constant market prices per person employed.

Source: *European Economy*, vol. 42, 1989; and vol. 55, 1993

undoubtedly claim the credit for the improved growth rate which followed, although growth remained lower than the EU average.

What is beyond doubt is that the depth of the recession in the UK in the early 1990s can be blamed on two British government mistakes. (In the EU over this period there has been a much milder recession.)

By 1986, a rapidly rising balance of payments deficit demonstrated that demand was growing faster than the ability of UK firms to expand supplies, the gap being filled by imports. Nevertheless further huge increases in demand were to come. In the 1988 budget, large income tax cuts were supposed to lead to expanded output through increased incentives. Chancellor Lawson said in his budget speech:

> '... The way to a strong economy is to boost incentives and enterprise. And that means, among other things, keeping income tax as low as possible. Excessive rates of income tax destroy enterprise.'

There may be some truth in this proposition, but the tax changes expanded *aggregate demand* far more than they increased *aggregate supply*, thus raising prices – the rate of inflation – and sucking in even more imports.

To combat the surge in inflation, interest rates were raised progressively, from 7.5 per cent in May 1988 to 15 per cent in October 1989, at which extremely high level they stayed for the next twelve months. In October 1990 the interest rate was reduced by one percentage point and simultaneously the then Chancellor, Mr John Major, took sterling into the ERM at too high an exchange rate. His successor as Chancellor, Mr Norman Lamont, ended up trying to defend an overvalued pound at its ERM-fixed rate.

If a rate is to be maintained against the judgements of the markets, it has to be by increasing the rate of interest. *So interest rates remained high although the domestic economy desperately needed them to be reduced.* During the boom of 1986–88 firms and businesses had borrowed heavily, house prices had also boomed and many people had taken out large mortgages. Soon all were to find their repayments hugely swollen by the unexpectedly high interest rates. Consumers cut back their expenditures, investment fell, firms and businesses began to go bankrupt with consequent job losses, leading to further falls in demand. As many people lost their firms, businesses, jobs and homes the government maintained high interest rates to hold the exchange rate of sterling in the ERM.

Eventually, large-scale speculators realized that the sterling exchange rate could not be held and enormous capital flows began. The Prime Minister and the Chancellor of the Exchequer both made public announcements that the rate of exchange would be maintained. The ERM system permits countries in such a situation to agree a devaluation of their currencies, but the British government chose not to do this, preferring to pour huge sums into the foreign exchanges before having to admit ignominious defeat. One speculator, made a profit of £650 million. The losses made by the British government, on behalf of taxpayers, were extremely large. Sterling was forced out of the ERM in September 1992.

Subsequent reductions in interest rates have been very welcome, but recovery from a recession of the depth which they caused will be slow. Even at the end of 1993, house repossessions were reported to exceed 1000 per week.

The above account of the UK economy's performance makes it clear that membership of the EU is no panacea; *it leaves much scope for national incompetence.* But surely other governments are also less than perfect and the UK economy should not be examined in isolation. How does it compare with the EU average?

In 1960 the UK enjoyed substantially higher GDP per head (incomes) than the average of the other members. By the time of accession the UK had lost this advantage. But by the 1980s the relative decline seemed to have been arrested – until the current recession.

Such data must be interpreted with care. It is impossible to prove that these economic changes are due to good or bad British government economic policies, or that membership of the EU is responsible. Obviously it is also impossible to counter the assertion that the UK would have performed better outside the Union. However, the continuation of trends between 1960 and accession would, by 1994, have reduced the UK's relative GDP to about 60 per cent of that of our neighbours. *Far from this happening, UK relative GDP has varied around the EU average since accession. This supports (but does not prove) the hypothesis that membership has been very beneficial.*

Chapter 2 discussed the theoretical background to economic integration. It concluded that the major economic benefit was the gain from trade resulting from the exploitation of comparative advantage, specialization and associated economies of size. How has UK trade with the EU progressed since accession? In terms of goods – **visible trade** – about one-third of UK imports and exports were traded with the EU immediately before accession; this share had gradually increased to 50 per cent of imports and 56 per cent of exports by 1991.

Figure 4 (overleaf) shows that the balance of trade has been markedly in favour of the EU during most of the period of UK

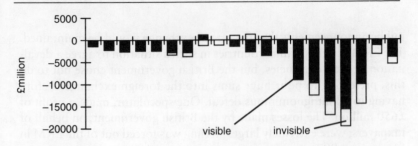

Figure 4 The UK's balance of trade with the EU, 1973–92

membership, and that the UK's trade balance deteriorated very rapidly in the latter half of the 1980s.

The UK government's mistakes contributing to this situation were discussed above, but there is another possible factor – the output of **North Sea oil** increased very quickly at the end of the 1970s to reach a peak in 1985. In only a few years the UK turned from being a major oil importer to being more than self-sufficient. This caused a swift rise in the sterling exchange rate, making British exports relatively expensive, and imports correspondingly cheap. Throughout the 1980s this effect was exacerbated by government reliance on high interest rates to control inflation which also forced up the exchange rate. As we have seen, this was particularly so from 1988 onwards. The UK's poor competitive position resulted in a rapid decline in manufacturing industry. Under such circumstances it is not surprising that the UK balance of *visible* trade with the EU has been so one-sided.

Even in **invisibles**, where the UK is supposed to have a comparative advantage, the deficit has been growing. However, major categories of invisibles, such as financial services, have been subject to NTBs preventing the exploitation of comparative advantage. As these sectors have been a major target of the Single Market programme, the position should improve in future.

It must be admitted that the growing size of the trade deficit since 1986 has been largely due to UK economic mismanagement as discussed earlier in the chapter.

The problem of agriculture

The much-criticized common agricultural policy has had four major negative influences on the UK.

Misallocation of resources

Agriculture has been more heavily protected than the manufacturing sector, so significant **resource misallocation** has occurred. Resources used by agriculture could have been used more productively in other sectors. High food prices push up labour costs and reduce international competitiveness. Dumping surpluses on world markets helps to reduce the costs of some competitors (Japan is a major food importer), and makes other food exporters poorer, thus reducing their demand for UK and other EU exports.

Trade diversion
Trade diversion is of considerable importance. Before accession the UK purchased food imports at low world market prices. Since accession, much food has been purchased from other member countries at the considerably higher internal prices.

Support costs
The budgetary costs of supporting European agriculture have fallen disproportionately heavily upon the UK. The UK has to contribute its share of expenditure, much of which pays for the disposal of agricultural surpluses produced by other members. Table 10 (overleaf) shows that UK payments to the budget have greatly exceeded receipts. The unfair budget mechanism resulted in some refunds to the UK being negotiated annually from 1980. Since 1985 these have been calculated according to a formula: the rebate to be 66 per cent of the difference between the UK's share of VAT contributions and its share of expenditure. The GNP-related budget resource introduced in 1988 is included in the rebate formula. However, the UK is still a major net contributor to the budget. Between 1973 and 1992 the cumulative net contribution exceeds £17 billion at current market prices; in constant 1994 prices it would be very much more. UK government estimates put the current net contributions at very nearly £2 billion per year.

If the reform of the CAP, noted in Chapter 4, reduces price support to give protection levels near to those accorded to manufacturing industry, then the problems identified so far in this section will be solved.

Environmental costs
High cereal prices persuaded farmers to plough much of the chalk downs, which at world prices would have remained in traditional grazing. So grasslands rich in wildlife – flowers, butterflies, and birds etc. – became cornfields whose production added to cereal surpluses. This is but one illustration of an extensive catalogue of unnecessary environmental degradation caused by the CAP's past high-price

Table 10 UK transactions with the EU budget, 1973–92 (£million)

	1973	1974	1975	1976	1977	1978	1979	1980	1981	1982	1983	1984	1985	1986	1987	1988	1989	1990	1991	1992
Credits																				
Agricultural fund	63	112	342	207	181	329	371	550	683	791	1082	1353	1151	1385	1345	1379	1315	1496	1761	1813
Social fund	–	16	19	11	48	63	87	95	107	152	128	283	256	335	428	277	406	225	618	437
Regional fund	–	–	–	29	60	35	71	173	145	111	139	184	274	298	404	370	347	441	370	551
Budget refunds[a]	–	–	–	–	–	–	–	98	693	1019	807	528	61	–	–	–	–	–	–	–
Other	17	25	38	52	88	107	136	154	152	186	172	197	172	198	168	156	48	21	17	22
Total credits	80	153	400	299	376	533	666	1070	1780	2259	2328	2545	1914	2216	2345	2182	2116	2183	2766	2823
Debits																				
Agricultural and sugar levies	9	14	32	38	154	242	247	260	218	307	232	260	189	244	354	226	192	135	205	206
Customs duties	142	192	320	438	613	714	868	861	861	1001	1075	1276	1291	1244	1417	1522	1638	1555	1529	1558
VAT & Fourth resource	–	–	–	–	–	596	844	741	1095	1497	1712	1720	1930	2742	3347	2886	3446	4149	4610	5291
VAT abatements[b]	–	–	–	–	–	–	–	–	–	–	–	–	–166	–1701	–1153	–1595	–1156	–1697	–2497	–1881
Adjustments[c]	–	–33	–11	–13	–30	–204	–352	–95	–	57	–43	–55	145	263	84	–127	311	516	–538	–317
Special agreements	–	–	–	–	–	–	–	–	–	–	–	–	370	–	–	613	–	–	–	–
Total debits	151	173	341	463	737	1348	1606	1767	2170	2862	2976	3201	3759	2792	4049	3525	4431	4658	3309	4857
Balance	–71	–20	59	–164	–361	–815	–940	–697	–390	–603	–648	–656	–1845	–576	–1704	–1343	–2315	–2475	–543	–2034

Notes: [a] Refunds negotiated annually.
[b] Abatements according to an agreed formula.
[c] UK share of adjustments required to balance budgets of previous years.

Sources: CSO 'Pink Books', various years.

regime. Unfortunately it is very difficult to recapture lost habitats, and impossible to recreate lost species, so the reformed CAP does not represent a return to paradise lost.

Summary
How much the CAP has cost the UK is unknown. The four costs identified fall into three types. The simplest is that of budgetary transfers which are exactly known. More difficult are the costs of trade diversion and resource misallocation which can only be estimated in relation to various assumptions.

A further degree of difficulty is associated with estimating environmental costs – how can you value wild flowers, butterflies or a beautiful view? Politicians tend to ignore all but the budgetary costs of the CAP, and take decisions related only to these.

Other environmental benefits
Environmental 'goods' and 'bads' are difficult to estimate, but they are nevertheless very important to our standard of living. On many of these issues common action is essential because action by individual nations is unlikely.

Acid rain is a good example. Its major source is coal-burning electricity power stations. Coal always contains some sulphur. When it is burnt, sulphurous gases enter the atmosphere appearing later in acid rain which corrodes public buildings (especially those built of limestone), acidifies lakes causing the death of fish, and harms large areas of pine forest in northern Europe. Removing the sulphurous gases from power station smoke is expensive, and so increases the costs of generating electricity. No government will want to see its costs rise by unilaterally introducing desulphurization. That the UK is currently building its first power station desulphurization plants is due to EU pressure, not UK enthusiasm.

Common action is also apparent in respect of *water pollution*. Much has been heard of the need for the UK to clean up its drinking water and its beaches. It is gradually being forced to do so by EU legislation despite UK government reluctance

Conclusion: is membership of the EU a good thing?
At the time of writing the UK has been a member for 20 years. Has membership been of net economic benefit so far, and what of the future?

Looking at the past, a conclusion is surprisingly difficult. The most widely known consequence of membership is the high budgetary costs to the UK of the CAP. Other costs and benefits are difficult to estimate.

One pointer, already mentioned above, is that prior to membership the UK's GDP was growing more slowly than the average for the Union, but has more recently kept pace. Unfortunately such information is capable of very different interpretations; it might be argued, for example, that outside the Union the UK's relative economic decline could have been reversed more effectively. No definitive answer to these questions is possible.

It is, perhaps, too soon to attempt to assess whether membership of the Union is economically beneficial to the UK. The Single Market is too recent for its expected substantial benefits to have been achieved yet. *But if the economic analysis of Chapter 2 is valid, then the UK will benefit in the long run – unless of course the UK becomes a depressed region, which is a possibility raised by the analysis of Chapter 5.*

KEY WORDS

Sovereignty	Resource misallocation
Visible trade	Trade diversion
North Sea oil	Environmental costs
Invisibles	Environmental benefits

Reading list

National Institute of Economic and Social Research (NIESR), *The UK Economy*, 2nd edn, Heinemann Educational, 1993 (particularly Chapters 6 and 7).

Paisley, R. and Quillfeldt, J., Chapter 35 in *Economics Investigated*, vol. 2, Collins Educational, 1992.

Essay topics

1. Discuss whether the benefits for the United Kingdom of the Single European Market are likely to exceed the costs. (Associated Examining Board, 1992)
2. Analyse the factors which have led to the deindustrialization of the UK economy since 1970. Discuss whether the completion of a Single European Market will accelerate deindustrialization. (Joint paper, Oxford & Cambridge SEB/Cambridge LES, AS Level, 1991)
3. What are the implications for the British economy of the completion of the Single European Market? (Oxford & Cambridge Schools Examination Board, 1992)

4. Explain the distinction between tariff and non-tariff barriers to trade. Discuss the likely impact of the single European market on the UK economy. (University of London Examinations and Assessment Council, 1991)

Data Response Question 7
The European car market

This task is based on a question set by the University of Oxford Delegacy of Local Examinations in 1992. Read the two articles below which are both adapted from pieces that appeared in national newspapers, and answer the questions that follow.

THE gap in prices between Britain and the rest of the European Community is growing wider, with British motorists paying up to a third more than motorists across the Channel, even though an EC ruling states that the price differential across the EC should not be more than 12 per cent.

A report by the Bureau of European Consumers' Unions found that the pre-tax price on one particular model was fixed at £4,486 in Denmark and then rose steadily in other EC countries until it reached a peak of £7,711 in Britain.

The price gap is leading to a resurgence of interest in importing cars privately from the Continent. The trail of bargain-hunters is now becoming large enough for manufacturers and distributors to start worrying about the effect on the price of the costly British car.

The European consumers' report found that, in an attempt to stem the tide, some British distributors were refusing to honour guarantees on privately imported cars, and dealers on the Continent, said to be acting on the instructions of manufacturers, were refusing to supply right-hand drive models for British customers.

Source: Adapted from 'Driving a bargain across the Channel', *Independent on Sunday*, 10 March 1990

The number of Japanese cars that can be bought in Britain will more than double under an agreement that is expected to be approved by the European Commission and Japan.

The move signals an end to a **voluntary quota system** that has protected British manufacturers since the mid-1970s. The revised import ceilings, which prepare the way for 1992 and the Single European Market, are much higher than expected.

Japanese manufacturers have **already secured a foothold in Britain** to prepare for rapid expansion into Europe. Nissan, the first company to establish a factory in the UK, will be followed by Toyota and Honda later this year. Within five years the Japanese will produce about 600,000 cars a year in Britain. The Japanese are able to circumvent import restrictions by setting up these 'transplant' factories.

The benefits to the consumer of the economies of scale have already been proved in America, where Japanese companies have captured about 30% share of the market. Many of the cars are nearly a third cheaper than similar models sold in Britain.

Source: Adapted from 'Japanese deal will slash car prices', *Sunday Times*, 23 Sept. 1990

1. (i) What is price discrimination? (ii) Is there any evidence in the first article which might lead you to suppose that price discrimination is being practised in the car industry? (iii) What economic explanation is there for the stated actions of distributors and dealers?
2. Why might pre-tax car prices in Britain be higher than in the European Union?
3. What has motivated Japanese car manufacturers to have 'already secured a foothold in Britain'.
4. Outline and comment on the potential benefits and costs to Britain, and Britain's European partners, of Japanese car manufacturers' investment in Britain and the ending of 'a voluntary quota system'.

Conclusion

All for one and one for all – Dumas

When one now observes the progress of economic and political integration in the European Union, it is difficult to believe that 50 years ago most of its members were in the depths of the Second World War. That war involved the four largest EU members as some of the main antagonists, two on one side, two on the other. It was separated from a similar preceding war by only one generation. If the coming together in the European Union of these previously warring factions had no other effect than to prevent a further war, the Union would be a great economic success, for even ignoring the terrible human costs, the economic waste of those two wars was enormous.

The prevention of war seems a rather negative benefit; this chapter now looks at the positive side where *all for one and one for all* is becoming literally true through the process of economic integration. We must look at the economic progress which has been achieved and the prospects for further progress in a Europe of rapid and accelerating change.

The economic success of the Union

During the past 30 years the economies of the twelve have grown more rapidly than that of the USA. As Table 11 shows, in 1960 the GDP per

Table 11 GDP per head: EU compared with USA and Japan, 1960–93

	EUR12 = 100	
	USA	Japan
1960	183.7	54.5
1965	175.8	66.6
1970	159.5	89.6
1975	151.3	93.0
1980	146.9	97.2
1985	148.4	106.4
1990	139.6	112.7
1993	140.3	118.0

The comparison is in terms of purchasing power parity
Source: *European Economy, 55,* 1993

head in the USA was nearly 84 per cent higher than that in the EU, but by 1993 the American lead was reduced to about 40 per cent. Over the same period Japanese GDP per head has rocketed from being 54 per cent of that in the EU to gaining a lead of 18 per cent. The report on European economic progress must be 'fairly good but could do better!'

Economic growth has been very variable during the Union's first three decades. Table 12 shows that initially growth was rapid; but worldwide recessions, largely caused by oil price shocks in 1974 and again in 1979, greatly reduced growth, and led to the under-employment of resources in general and labour in particular. After 1984, growth began to accelerate but unemployment, although falling, remained high compared with the 1960s.

The improvements in the 1980s can be attributed to three main factors:

- success in controlling inflation
- the implementation of supply-side policies
- introduction of the Single Market.

As noted in Chapter 3 there are still some NTBs – notably differences in tax and excise duty rates – distorting competition and hindering the operation of comparative advantage. But these factors are not sufficient to explain the slowdown since the beginning of the 1990s – economic growth has slowed, and unemployment has risen. The Commission blames an undeserved loss of confidence. Within Europe the 1990 German reunification was far more expensive than expected, and simultaneously the recession in the UK rapidly deepened. *It is*

Table 12 EU – some economic indicators, 1961–93

	1961 to 1973	1974 to 1985	1986	1987	1988	1989	1990	1991	1992	1993*
GDP annual real growth rate (%)	4.8	2.0	2.9	2.9	4.2	3.5	3.0	1.4	1.0	–0.6
Gross investment (as % GDP)	23.2	21.1	19.0	19.3	20.1	20.8	20.9	20.3	19.6	18.6
Employment change (annual %)	0.3	0	0.7	1.2	1.5	1.5	1.7	0.2	–0.6	–1.7
Inflation rate (%)	4.7	10.8	3.8	3.6	3.8	5.0	4.5	5.4	4.4	3.7
Unemployment (%)	2.1	6.8	10.7	10.4	9.8	8.9	8.3	8.7	9.3	10.4

* Forecast.
Source: *European Economy*, 55, 1993.

probable that such problems in two of the largest economies of the Union have been significant factors in the slowdown which has affected all twelve EU economies.

The Delors White Paper, detailed in Chapter 5, gives the Commission's long-term plans for accelerating economic growth, one of the main objectives of which is to reduce unemployment. The financial costs of unemployment are estimated by the Commission to be about £155 billion a year.

Appraisal of EU economic strategy

It is interesting that the Commission has been formulating long-term plans for the last 35 years and is continuing to do so. This is in marked contrast to the UK government attitude prevalent over the last 15 years; here, investment decisions have been regarded as the sole prerogative of firms and businesses operating in a free market.

The 1992 EU budget provided nearly 2 bn Ecu (about £1.5 billion) for research and development, concentrated particularly on high technology areas. Is such public intervention in research more effective (in terms of economic growth) than leaving it to industry?

The experiences of Japan and the USA provide some pointers. Japanese leadership in many areas of technology has resulted from many years of public intervention, with huge expenditures being targeted on correctly identified growth areas. High growth rates in the USA since the Second World War have been attributed to civil spinoffs from gigantic military research programmes; for example, the original Boeing airliner, the first major successful jet airliner, came from a very expensively developed military aircraft. The slower USA growth rate of the last decade correlates with the rapid reduction of military research expenditures – suggesting that the market alone is not the best deliverer of economic growth even in the most capitalistic of cultures.

The EU in a wider Europe

When three of the European Free Trade Area countries (Denmark, Ireland, UK) joined the European Community in 1973, the remaining EFTA countries (Austria, Finland, Iceland, Norway, Sweden, Switzerland and Portugal – with the later loss of Portugal and gain of Liechtenstein) negotiated a free trade agreement with the Community. In 1992 the Community and EFTA agreed to the creation of the European Economic Area (EEA). This expanded the earlier free trade arrangements to include the free movement of labour, services and capital, but the EFTA countries in return had to adopt almost all of the existing Community legislation except that relating to agriculture or

Figure 5 The EU and EFTA

border controls. In future they will be consulted on further EU legislation but will have no right to vote. The EEA came into force on 1 January 1994 for the EFTA countries – excluding Switzerland, which rejected the closer association in a referendum, and Liechtenstein because of its close ties with Switzerland; for the latter two countries the previous free trade arrangements still apply. The EEA is the world's largest integrated economic area, having a total population exceeding 370 millions and covering the whole of western Europe (see Figure 5).

The current EEA relationship between EFTA and EU is changing as most EFTA members are joining the EU. Formal negotiations with Austria, Finland, Norway and Sweden opened in November 1993 and were completed in March 1994; the applicants become new members on 1 January 1995. What happened to the fifth EFTA country to join the EEA? Iceland feared a loss of control over its fishing grounds and decided not to seek 'promotion' from the EEA.

In southern Europe, membership applications have been received (chronologically) from Turkey, Cyprus and Malta. It is instructive to consider the Turkish application in some detail. Turkey negotiated an association agreement (basically freer trade) with the Community in 1963; this was intended to develop into a full customs union relationship possibly by 1995 with full membership following by 1997. But in 1989 the Commission published an opinion which effectively postponed any closer integration for the foreseeable future. The reasons given were that Turkey had a large and rapidly expanding population (more than 60 million), a weak economy and lower living standards than any part of the Community – indeed, large areas were considered to be at Third World levels of development. The Commission judged that Turkey would be unable to adjust economically or politically. Finally, the Turkish invasion of northern Cyprus, which has divided the island into a Turkish north and Greek south, guarantees that, until the division is reversed, at least one current member of the EU will veto Turkish accession.

It should be noted that the Turkish application is postponed rather than rejected: the strategic position of Turkey between east and west, and its long defence and institutional relations with the EU, make outright rejection highly undesirable.

Cyprus negotiated an association agreement in 1972 and applied in 1990 for full membership, but the division of the island prevents further progress. Malta has had an association agreement since 1970 and also applied in 1990 for full membership; there are no major difficulties and early membership seems probable.

To the east, the collapse of Communism has led to association agreements with Czechoslovakia, Hungary and Poland. Their ultimate membership, however, must be distant. Like Turkey, their economies are very weak and living standards are very low. Full membership will be a long time coming if only because it includes the free movement of labour which would result in mass uncontrolled 'economic migration'.

Other east European countries – those outside the new Commonwealth comprising the major countries of the old Soviet bloc – are also attracted economically and politically to the EU. They see full membership of the EU as an essential safeguard to their independence as well as helping their progress towards becoming market economies.

In the interest of political stability as well as economic development, many consider that the EU should offer some long-term arrangement which would give these countries a realistic expectation of full membership in time. It is argued that very lengthy transitions to full membership are better than leaving countries to the sort of destructive nationalism and poverty which may otherwise develop. The fate of Yugoslavia supports this argument.

What about Russia? It is generally accepted that Russia, even if it wished to join, is too big to be absorbed into the EU. In terms of population it is half the size of the current Union, whilst geographically it stretches from western Europe to the Pacific. Consequently any future relationship between the EU and Russia, along with its Commonwealth partners, is likely to be constrained to aid and cooperation.

Conclusion

Over the years the European Union has developed from its original six members to nine, to ten, to twelve, soon to sixteen and still more countries wish to join. Clearly in the eyes of many the Union is a success. The continuing development of the Single Market promises to further enhance the Union's economy – already it is the world's largest developed country market in terms of population and, as Adam Smith observed, 'specialization is limited by the extent of the market' – meaning that efficiency depends on market size. The Community has the potential to become, within a generation, the world's major economic power.

The Treaty of Maastricht attempts to further the process of making *all into one* by emphasizing political integration as well as economic integration. Indeed, the former is essential to the progress of economic and monetary union. But there is a conflict between this deepening of the current Union and its widening to include (except the current EEA applicants) many much poorer countries. Ultimately the Union could treble its current membership of countries and double its current population. Reconciling the deepening/widening conflict is a challenge which the Union must accept.

Further reading

Healey, N.M., Chapter 5 in *Britain's Economic Miracle*, Routledge, 1993.

Index